# Praise for *Transformative Language Arts in Action*

"When you take writers and poets into areas where real people are dealing with real life problems and traumas, with humble joys, renewing their hope in life, having expressive breakthroughs—that is the gift to all of us. It allows real people to tell their stories, to share their grief and gratitude, to untwist the dark silence that wraps their hearts and lengthen it out into a sonnet, a narrative poem, a celebratory lyric—that is essentially what language and words are for.

What these writers have done is nothing short of challenging the stale models of writing to and for other writers; other poets entrenched in the moldy hallways of academia. When writing breaks down the doors, when writing is used to really reach across the dark chasm and speak out, call by name the ghosts that lurk there and invoke one's own power with fearless defiance, well then, that is truly writing from the heart, writing that is mapped and charted to define and explore our human experience. That is what this book does, and I applaud the editors, writers, and poets. So impressive is this volume that every high school child and every citizen should have it in their backpacks and book shelves." —**Jimmy Santiago Baca**, poet and author, *A Glass of Water* and *Singing at the Gates*; founder, Cedar Tree, Inc.

"This is as much a testimonial to the resilience and creativity of the human spirit as it is an informative exploration of an emerging field, transformative language arts. A collection of reflections, stories, and reports on the work of change agents whose medium is language (whether spoken, written, sung, enacted, or remembered), it shares with us the many ways people are successfully being moved to write, being heard into speech, and being liberated into action through the work of these caring professionals." —**Elizabeth Minnich**, professor, Queens University (moral philosophy); author, *Transforming Knowledge*

"A transformation awaits each reader in this volume's wealth of language, heart, scholarship, and stories within stories to inspire action in whatever small way we can to affect our large, troubled yet beautiful world. Each contributor is a 'change agent' who creatively points the way to a higher level of understanding of our varied fellow human beings through language's many avenues leading to hope and survival." —**Perie Longo**, Poet Laureate Emerita, Santa Barbara, CA; registered poetry therapist; author, *Baggage Claim*

"This new anthology of transformative language arts (TLA) essays highlights the excitement of this emerging field. Founded as a master of arts program at Goddard College, TLA has spread across the country as a cutting edge practice in the arts, ecology, business, activism, and health. Ruth Farmer and Caryn Mirriam-Goldberg bring together leading voices to demonstrate how words have power to change individual lives as well as communities. Join with them to help catalyze social change." —**Denise Low**, Kansas Poet Laureate, 2007–2009

"This book is about how words can change lives, and in so doing, change the world. From stories of homeless women finding their voice to the power of song to transform inner life, this is a book that revives the ancient awareness of the dynamic energy of language. What an antidote this book is to the popular media's silence and silliness in the face of injustice." —**Barbara Kerr**, distinguished professor of counseling psychology and director, CLEOS (Counseling Laboratory for the Exploration of Optimal States), University of Kansas

"Having already been familiar with Farmer and Mirriam-Goldberg's teaching and work, I am thrilled to see this book actualize the remarkable teaching and pedagogy they both advocate. This collection not only moves you to rethink your teaching practices with its understanding of 'communities of congruence,' but invites you to investigate methodologies that alter the stale modes of workshop and creative writing teaching and the possibilities of teaching outside the classroom—the rest of the world and its places of nurture, hardship, and recovery." —**Prageeta Sharma**, professor, University of Montana; author, *Undergloom* and *Infamous Landscapes*

"Now one could argue that it was merely a creative writing class and you would be right, but what is teaching creative writing but teaching creative thought? And from imagination springs dreams." —Participant in the transformative language arts writing workshop, "A Circle of Women, a Circle of Words"

"The chapters in this groundbreaking anthology provide artists, educators, activists, scholars, community organizers, and spiritual leaders with a blueprint for applying the spoken, written, and/or sung word for initiating personal and social transformation. Leading artists, educators, and practitioners within the emerging field describe concrete ways to present workshops, performances, and other community activities that engage participants in the process of self-discovery, creative expression, and community building. Whether working with women subsisting in housing projects or people combating mental illness or cancer patients and caregivers living with the profound impact of the illness, the contributors share their experiences as testimonials to the life-changing power of these practices." —**Michelle Myers**, spoken word artist; founder of Yellow Rage; activist; professor

# Transformative Language Arts in Action

*Also in the It's Easy to W.R.I.T.E. Expressive Writing Series*

*Writing with At-Risk Youth: The Pongo Teen Writing Method*
Richard Gold

*Expressive Writing: Foundations of Practice*
Edited by Kathleen Adams

*The Flourishing Principal: Strategies for Self-Renewal*
Kathleen Adams and Rosemary Lohndorf

*The Teacher's Journal: A Workbook for Self-Discovery*
Kathleen Adams and Marisé Barreiro

# Transformative Language Arts in Action

EDITED BY RUTH FARMER AND
CARYN MIRRIAM-GOLDBERG

ROWMAN & LITTLEFIELD
*Lanham • Boulder • New York • London*

Published by Rowman & Littlefield
A wholly owned subsidiary of The Rowman & Littlefield Publishing Group, Inc.
4501 Forbes Boulevard, Suite 200, Lanham, Maryland 20706
www.rowman.com

Unit A, Whitacre Mews, 26–34 Stannary Street, London SE11 4AB, United Kingdom



British Library Cataloguing in Publication Information Available

**Library of Congress Cataloging-in-Publication Data Available**
ISBN 978-1-4758-1059-2 (cloth : alk. paper)—ISBN 978-1-4758-1060-8 (pbk. : alk. paper)—ISBN 978-1-4758-1061-5 (electronic)

∞™ The paper used in this publication meets the minimum requirements of American National Standard for Information Sciences—Permanence of Paper for Printed Library Materials, ANSI/NISO Z39.48-1992.

Printed in the United States of America

# Contents

Series Overview: About the *It's Easy to W.R.I.T.E.* Expressive Writing Series ix

Introduction: "To Speak a True Word Is to Change the World" xiii
*Ruth Farmer and Caryn Mirriam-Goldberg*

1 A Snake in the Grass: Challenges of Dominant Stories 1
*James Sparrell*

**Snapshot:** Sherry Reiter, poetry therapy pioneer, educator, clinical social worker, writer, storyteller 14

**Snapshot:** Seema Reza, recreational arts program coordinator at military hospitals, poet, and writer 16

2 "Everyone's Life Is a Book": Public Housing Women Write for Their Lives 19
*Caryn Mirriam-Goldberg*

**Snapshot:** Vanita Leatherwood, writer, facilitator, and director of sexual assault and domestic violence center 39

**Snapshot:** Heather Severson, writer, workshop model developer, and facilitator 40

**3** Holding the Space: TLA Values in Education 41
*Ruth Farmer*

**Snapshot:** Patricia Fontaine, writer and facilitator of workshops for people living with cancer 57

**Snapshot:** Nancy Morgan, Arts and Humanities Director at Georgetown Lombardi Comprehensive Cancer Center 58

**4** Youth, Writing, and Identity: An Interview with Sarah W. Bartlett 59
*Ruth Farmer*

**Snapshot:** Suzanne Adams, workshop facilitator for adolescent girls, and writer 77

**Snapshot:** Minna Dubin, workshop facilitator for women and youth, writer 78

**5** Zamlers, Tricksters, and Queers: Re-Mixing Histories in Yiddishland and Faerieland 79
*Ezra Berkley Nepon*

**Snapshot:** Miriam Gabriel, blogger and spoken-word artist 94

**Snapshot:** Ruth Gendler, writer, artist, and facilitator of workshops for children and adults 95

**6** Performing for Social Change: Interviews with Kao Kue, Taína Asili, and Katt Lissard 97
*Ruth Farmer*

**Snapshot**: Kelley Hunt, singer-songwriter, international touring and teaching artist 122

**Snapshot:** Deb Hensley, singer-songwriter, writer, consultant, facilitator, and TLA Network coordinator 123

**7** Theopoetics as a Spiritual Form of Transformative Language Arts 125
*Callid Keefe-Perry*

**Snapshot:** Larry Greer, interfaith minister and pastoral coordinator 139

**Snapshot:** Joanna Tebbs Young, writer, columnist, expressive writing and spirituality workshop facilitator, and workshop developer 140

**8** Women's Self-Leadership through Transformative Narratives 143
*Yvette Angelique Hyater-Adams*

**Snapshot**: Lisa McIvor, home health nurse, workshop facilitator for people with disabilities, poet and writer 156

**Snapshot**: Jen Cross, writer and erotic writer, facilitator of workshops for survivors of sexual violence and for erotic writing 158

**Snapshot:** Angie River, spoken-word and burlesque artist 160

**9** Autobiography of a Social Body 161
*Juliana Borrero*

**Snapshot**: Richard Hodgson, writer, storyteller, and workshop facilitator for elders 182

**Snapshot**: Scott Youmans, seminarian, web consultant, writer, and facilitator 183

**10** Deep Connection: Healing Self, Others, and Nature through Transformative Language Arts 185
*Brian W. Sunset*

Resources 201

About the Editors and Contributors 203

# Series Overview: About the *It's Easy to W.R.I.T.E.* Expressive Writing Series

Expressive writing originates from the writer's lived experience—past, present, or imagined future life. Written in the author's own voice, expressive writing creates bridges between thought and feeling, reason and intuition, idea and action. It is equally rooted in language arts and social science, and it takes multiple forms: journals, poetry, life story, personal essay, creative nonfiction, song lyrics, notes, and snippets of thought. Expressive writing is democratic and accessible. No special knowledge is needed, supplies are available and affordable, and research confirms that outcomes can be profound and even life-changing.

The *It's Easy to W.R.I.T.E.* Expressive Writing Series captures the voices of worldwide experts on the power of writing for personal development, academic improvement, and lasting behavioral change. Authors are both theorists and practitioners of the work they document, bringing real-life examples of practical techniques and stories of actual outcomes.

Individually or as a compendium, the volumes in the *It's Easy to W.R.I.T.E.* Expressive Writing Series represent thoughtful, innovative, demonstrated approaches to the myriad ways life-based writing can shape both critical thinking and emotional intelligence. Books in the series are designed to have versatile appeal for classroom teachers and administrators, health and behavioral health professionals, graduate programs that prepare educators and counselors, facilitators of expressive writing, and individuals who themselves write expressively. Workbooks offer well-crafted, self-paced writing programs for individual users, with facilitation guides and curricula for anyone who wishes to organize peer-writing circles to explore the material in community.

Each book or chapter author is held to exacting standards set by the series editor, Kathleen Adams, who, prior to her 1985 launch as a pioneer and global expert in the expressive writing field, was trained as a journalist and served as chief editor for a nonfiction publishing company.

# It's Easy to W.R.I.T.E.

**W**hat do you want to write about? Name it. Write it down. (If you don't know, try one of these: *What's going on? How do I feel? What's on my mind? What do I want? What's the most important thing to do? What's the best/worst thing right now?*)

**R**econnect with your center. Close your eyes. Take three deep breaths. Focus. Relax your body and mind. Gather your thoughts, feelings, questions, ideas.

**I**nvestigate your thoughts and feelings. Start writing and keep writing. Follow the pen/keyboard. If you get stuck, close your eyes and recenter yourself. Reread what you've already written and continue. Try not to edit as you go; that can come later, if at all.

**T**ime yourself. Write for five to twenty minutes or whatever time you choose. Set the timer on your phone, stove, or computer. Plan another three to five minutes at the end for reflection.

**E**xit smart. Reread what you've written and reflect on it in a sentence or two: *As I read this, I notice* . . . or *I'm aware of* . . . or *I feel* . . . Note any action steps you might take or any prompts you might use for additional writes.

# Introduction

## "To Speak a True Word Is to Change the World"

Ruth Farmer and Caryn Mirriam-Goldberg

In the Hebrew tradition of Tikkun Olam—"repairing the world"—each of us has our work to do, our piece of the emerging mosaic of a better world. Whether working with the shards of whatever is wrong with the world (neglect, abuse, poverty, war, illness, oppression, ecological degradation) or celebrating the strengths found within individuals, families, communities, and cultures, we can draw on the power of words for the sake of the world. Transformative language arts (TLA), an emerging academic field, profession, and calling, offers us a way to perform Tikkun Olam, whether it's personal writing to cultivate greater clarity and courage, group storytelling to catalyze community empowerment, or collaborative performances to celebrate interfaith dialogue.

TLA draws on the potential of the written, spoken, and sung word to celebrate, liberate, and transform individuals and communities, ideas and culture, ways of knowing and vitality. TLA focuses on the river that runs through all forms of the spoken, written, and sung word for a purpose beyond entertainment or expression, bridging the gap between personal and societal health, growth, and change. This double focus in TLA—looking within and looking at who we are collectively—calls on us to contextualize our individual struggles, challenges, heartbreaks, and brokenness within societal, economic, historic, and ecological complexities and issues.

By using our words aloud (plays, storytelling, songs, spoken word, collaborative performance) or on the page (fiction, poetry, memoir, journaling, mixed-genre writing), we can also better understand how global forces affect our local lives and, from this perspective, better glimpse how to respond individually and collectively. Educator and activist Parker Palmer (2011) speaks of "communities of congruence" that help people to learn how to become change agents:

> Communities of congruence are like nurseries or hothouses where plants are tended until they are hearty enough to be transplanted outdoors and subjected to all kinds of weather. In a circle of trust, for example, participants are able to speak the vulnerable language of the heart in the presence of people who affirm it instead of tearing it down . . . As participants continue to make themselves vulnerable in a nurturing environment, the heart's language grows more robust and slowly becomes their "new normal." Eventually, the day comes when they find themselves speaking their hearts in public, having almost forgotten that doing so once seemed impossibly risky. (187)

Transformative language artists prioritize the creation of environments in which individuals can recognize their strengths, find their voices, and, ultimately, impact the communities in which they live and work.

While TLA as a term is a recent development, the essence of TLA recognizes the ancient impulse to tell our truths, which breaks silences of marginalized individuals and communities and gives voice to the expansive possibilities of human potential. At the same time, TLA embraces dualities that often separate vocations and avocations: the personal and the political, words aloud and on the page, individual and community arts and voice, the psychology of personal healing, and the social change of societal transformation.

Founded first through a master's program at Goddard College, TLA has grown several hubs around which people gather, network, and further develop the field and profession. In addition to the Goddard master's program in TLA, founded in 2000, the not-for-profit TLA Network organizes an annual conference, The Power of Words; the global One City One Prompt project; online classes; the professional and scholarly journal *Chyrsalis: A Journal of Transformative Language Arts*; and a new certification in TLA.

*The Power of Words: A TLA Reader*, co-edited by Caryn Mirriam-Goldberg and Janet Tallman, published in 2007 by the TLA Network, was the first anthology of TLA writings, and now we are happy to add this anthology to the body of literature on TLA. Because of the democratic nature of this emerging and interdisciplinary field, and because of the diverse ways of viewing TLA as a force for social change, we sought out writers who are change agents in various realms, including academia, activism, the arts, health, business, theology, and ecology.

In our contribution here, *Transformative Language Arts in Action*, the ways in which we frame the stories we live can open up or close down opportunities for expression and dialogue, as James Sparrell writes about in "A Snake in the Grass: Challenges of Dominant Stories." Changing how we frame stories, particularly the stories that tell us who we are and how we are to live, is central to understanding diverse ways of seeing the world. Beginning with two disparate perspectives on snakes, his grandfather's and his own, Sparrell shows how individual narratives create clashing worldviews, writing, "Narratives are a crucial way in which we organize ourselves in relation to the world, personally and culturally. Appreciating the ways in which our underlying schemas can limit us and keep us stuck provides a strategy for fundamentally shifting the stories we tell and the stories we live." A narrative therapist, educator, and writer, Sparrell brings to our book important considerations when it comes to shifting personal, communal, and cultural stories.

Caryn Mirriam-Goldberg's "'Everyone's life is a book': Public Housing Women Write for Their Lives" illustrates how changing the frame of a story can change lives. Her chapter highlights the power of writing for women who are on the financial and social edges: single mothers, elders, and middle-class women who have fallen on hard times. Additionally, Mirriam-Goldberg looks at how public housing women writing together incubated positive life changes for some participants. But in the context of mental illness, addiction, and other debilitating illnesses, sometimes writing in community exposes the brokenness in our culture more than it fixes that brokenness. Mirriam-Goldberg writes of the eight-year workshop series, "Learning to share with others such dreams, and witness their own, was central to what we did together in the workshop. Being witnessed helped the women feel the true weight of their words, and what they believed, needed, were ready for most at this point in their lives."

TLA principles can also flourish in our educational system. In "Holding Space: TLA Values in Education," Ruth Farmer investigates how TLA values are reflected in two college settings, at a private liberal arts college (Goddard College) and at a public community college (Community College of Vermont) when the process of writing as a way of knowing is given its necessary value and attention. As Farmer tells us, "Words might not save lives, but they certainly encourage us toward a broader understanding of and collaboration with various communities, which are the first steps toward meaningful social change."

In "Youth, Writing, and Identity" Ruth Farmer interviews Sarah W. Bartlett, director of Women Writing for (a) Change Vermont. They talk about how writing together can change and save the lives of girls and women. With ample examples of the collective and individual writing women and girls have done over the years in Bartlett's programs, she shows the power of finding and sharing our voices.

Taking individual and community voices into the realm of history is central to Ezra Berkley Nepon's chapter, "Zamlers, Tricksters, and Queers: Re-Mixing Histories in Yiddishland and Faerieland," which chronicles Nepon's research into the theatrical methodology of Jenny Romaine and members of the Eggplant Faerie Players, which led to creating a "people's history" that moves "beyond invisibility, nostalgia, or objectification." As a people's historian, Nepon also further develops TLA as a way to tell history, particularly about people creating transformative language art on the edges. As she writes,

> As we tell our stories and the stories of our cultures, and as that communication brings us towards personal and social transformation, aren't we also doing the work of people's history? Aren't the stories we tell also a kind of archive? If we understand our own stories and storytelling as meaningfully part of a collective

history, does that help us clarify how these stories can make change beyond the individual, catalyzing collective transformation?

Ruth Farmer's three-voice interview, "Performing for Social Change: Interviews with Kao Kue, Taína Asili, and Katt Lissard," further demonstrates TLA in action through the voices and experiences of a spoken word artist, singer-songwriter, and theater director/playwright. Drawing from various traditions—Kue from her Hmong community in the United States and Laos, Asili from her Puerto Rican roots, and Lissard from her theater projects in Lesotho and the United States—these interviews illustrate the myriad ways in which performance can save and share cultures, and catalyze effective individual and community change.

Such change is also at the forefront of Callid Keefe-Perry's "Theopoetics as a Spiritual Form of Transformative Language Arts," in which he explores TLA as spiritual practice in action. Keefe-Perry, a traveling minister, scholar, TLA activist, and performer, demonstrates the complementarity of theopoetics and TLA in their mutual evolution and cross-pollination as both helping "truth to prosper."

Looking toward how leadership begins with leading ourselves, Yvette Angelique Hyater-Adams writes about how what the Dalai Lama said about Western women saving the world may be true in complicated and important ways. In "Women's Self-Leadership through Transformative Narratives," Hyater-Adams calls for leadership informed by feminine values of collaboration, creativity, and nurturance, and she shares her transformative narratives model of using storytelling and poetry to help women discover their strengths and challenges as leaders. "Mapping out a self-leadership learning journey using transformative narratives can be a successful formula for women to meet our leadership development goals," she writes.

Modeling the rhythms and synthesized voices and ideas of the Language and Peace group, Juliana Borrero takes readers through the theoretical and practical applications of embodied writing in her chapter "Autobiography of a Social Body." Looking at what it means to write authentically individually and collectively, Borrero experiments with using language to dismantle what divides us and, instead, write our way toward inclusion, telling us:

> Language is a House for becoming our Selves. Now that we know this, we are called to participate in its building, because the House that we had lived in was

> like a prison, or there was no space for us, or we were homeless. We are building a big House with large empty spaces and a river singing next to it; where many others who didn't have a House will be welcome.

From the house of language, we go to the Earth that holds it all in Brian W. Sunset's "Deep Connection: Healing Self, Others, and Nature through Transformative Language Arts." Sunset gives us a view into his eco-TLA workshops, in which words offer "healing of individuals and their communities, including the broader ecological communities of which they are a part." He also shares examples of what kinds of personal transformations can happen from deepening our connection with the living Earth.

Interspersed throughout this book are glimpses into the professional lives of TLAers. Through these snapshots, readers will see the range of professions that encompass transformative language arts. Each snapshot highlights how a transformative language artist makes a living and makes a life, including poetry therapy pioneers, military hospital and cancer center program coordinators, domestic violence center directors, arts innovators, youth activists, writers, bloggers, spoken-word artists, singer-songwriters, consultants, coaches, nurses, ministers, burlesque artists, and workshop facilitators.

Central to all the chapters and snapshots in this book is the potential for words to intentionally change the world. Paulo Freire, a Brazilian educator and philosopher whose work *Pedagogy of the Oppressed* (2005) looks at the essence of words and change in a way that articulates this core of TLA:

> An unauthentic word, one which is unable to transform reality, results when dichotomy is imposed upon its constitutive elements. When a word is deprived of its dimension of action, reflection automatically suffers as well; and the word is changed into idle chatter, into verbalism, into an alienated and alienating "blah." It becomes an empty word, one which cannot denounce the world, for denunciation is impossible without a commitment to transform, and there is no transformation without action. . . . To speak a true word is to transform the world. (87)

TLA's focus on the speaking of true words, with the aim to change the world, rings through this collection.

# References

Freire, Paulo. 2005. *Pedagogy of the oppressed.* New York: Continuum.

Palmer, Parker J. 2011. *Healing the heart of democracy: The courage to create a politics worthy of the human spirit.* San Francisco: Jossey-Bass.

1

# A Snake in the Grass

## Challenges of Dominant Stories

James Sparrell

As a child, I spent many hours exploring the tall white pine woods around our house and the patchy lawns and garden beds that my dad had carved out with an old yellow bulldozer. He built our house on a piece of land that his father had given him. I discovered that by turning over a piece of granite or cement block, I could find millipedes and centipedes, and occasionally a red-backed salamander. But most of all, when I was seven or so, I had a strong attraction to snakes.

Our yard was home to common garter snakes with their beautiful black and greenish-yellow stripes. I wouldn't see them every day as I went around chasing bugs with my homemade butterfly net, but once in a while a garter snake would find a sunny spot, and we would startle each other for a moment. I discovered that if I picked one up, it would exude a pungent white substance, the scent of which was difficult to eradicate, even with multiple washings—which I was frequently directed to undertake. Eventually I learned to grab it gently near the head so I could scoop it up without getting anything on me.

It was at about this age that I acquired a copy of Robert Snedigar's book *Our Small Native Animals: Their Habits and Care*, originally published in 1939. I loved how Snedigar blurred the boundary between "animal" and "pet" by providing recommendations for what skunks or raccoons might need if one happened to obtain one for a pet. Today, I find the thought of transforming a "wild animal" into a pet disturbing, but in the spirit of the times and in my child-mind, it seemed like a brilliant idea. I started with a terrarium of red-striped salamanders and moved up to keeping a tub in the basement for the painted turtles I caught.

While going through Snedigar's impressive compendium of animals ranging from alligator lizards to great-horned owls, I came across his description of the hog-nosed snake and fell in a sort of seven-year-old love. He wrote about how the snake would begin by puffing up its body and threatening like a rattlesnake, but then ultimately "pretending injury, he rolls over and over, mouth wide open and snapping at his own body, till at last with a final shudder, he is on his back, forked tongue protruded and still. Quite convincingly the tail 'dies' last in a pathetic and convulsive twitch" (1963, 172). My mother put her foot down about snakes in the house, so I was not able to mail-order the hog-nosed snake that I had found advertised in the back of a magazine. My only hope in witnessing this drama was by finding one myself. I was on a quest.

This was several years after my grandmother had died, and it was my job to call my grandfather each night and invite him to dinner. Why we could not have a standing invitation for him to walk over and eat with us, I do not know. I had to pick up the big black handset and dial GA9-2924. I would say, "Hi, Grampa, it's Jimmy. Do you want to come to supper?" He would say, "Okay. What time?" as if the time might vary, but it didn't. "In about fifteen minutes." "Okay. Bye."

These were tense meals with our small family, since my grandfather and my father did not speak directly to each other or make eye contact. They would both make general pronouncements apparently directed at no one in particular but to the room, sometimes responding to what the other had said and sometimes not. Technical and mechanical questions about cars, motors, electrical, or plumbing systems might be posed to the air pertaining to single-phase and double-phase motors, the relative merits of alternating or direct current, or why the turn signal in the International Scout didn't turn off when my grandfather took the slight left turn onto High Street. My brother and I and my mother rarely found our way into these "conversations."

One night my grandfather reported that he had found a snake in his garden—just putting the discovery out there. I asked with excitement about what kind of snake it was and where it might be now. He had killed it—my brother later explained how he would hit them with a shovel. My grandfather must have seen my face, so profoundly sad, puzzled, and betrayed in our mutual passion for all wild things. My mother and brother later explained that he feared snakes and killed them almost instinctively. It was in this moment, although I would not have put it this way at the time, that I discovered that my grandfather and I had very different dominant single stories about snakes—his of fear, mine of love. I couldn't see what there was to be afraid of, but his general narrative of fascination with nature was blinded, in this instance, by gut terror.

While this is a personal example of dominant stories that are at odds, religious and political ideology, national identity, and cultural conflicts all suggest that there are many ways that groups, as well as individuals, find themselves at an impasse with each other as they inhabit these strong narratives.

## How Do We Construct and Maintain Stories?

In recent years, as neuropsychology and cognitive psychology have been exploring common domains, there has been an increased interest and focus on complex processes such as story construction and storytelling. Gazzaniga writes, "we don't just neutrally add up incoming information. Rather, nature designed our brains to devote a particular, and very significant region—the left brain—to the task of interpreting, and it reconciles our past and present knowledge to come up with ideas about the world around us" (2005, 137). He suggests even more strongly that "the left hemisphere makes strange input logical, it includes a special region that interprets the inputs we receive every moment and weaves them into stories to form the ongoing narrative of our self-image and our beliefs. I have called this area the interpreter because it seeks explanations for internal and external events and expands on the actual facts we experience to make sense of, or interpret, the events of our life" (148). Though today, many researchers would consider the distinction between left and right brain functioning as closer to metaphor, given that brains and bodies function in remarkably integrated ways, the idea that our bodies/brains fundamentally seek, create, and use stories to understand our experience can be helpful in understanding how we change or resist change, both as individuals and as societal groups.

In considering my grandfather's fear of snakes and my unequivocal fascination with them, it is an overstatement to call this a "story" in a traditional sense. There is no real plot and few characters. But to the extent that one of our encounters with a snake became a story, it is clear that the "interpreter," as Gazzaniga refers to it, exerted a powerful influence. The elements of stories have very deep roots within our bodies, and often we are not conscious of the kinds of simplifications, generalizations, and distortions that we may be making in order to "make sense" of information. They present themselves to us as simply and apparently "true."

In Gazzaniga's (2012) early "split-brain" research, he worked with people who had some of the primary pathways between left and right hemispheres surgically severed in order to decrease the frequency and intensity of the seizures they were experiencing, which could not be controlled in other ways. This may have exaggerated some of the differences he found, in terms of the clear distinctions between left and right hemispheres, but the results are still intriguing. He explains:

> We showed a split-brain patient two pictures: To his right visual field, a chicken claw, so the left hemisphere saw only the claw picture, and to the left visual field, a snow scene, so the right hemisphere saw only that. He was then asked to choose a picture from an array placed in full view in front of him, which both hemispheres could see. His left hand pointed to a shovel (which was the most appropriate answer for the snow scene) and his right hand pointed to a chicken (the most appropriate answer for the chicken claw).
>
> We asked why he chose those items. His left-hemisphere speech center replied, "Oh, that's simple. The chicken claw goes with the chicken," easily explaining what it knew. It had seen the chicken claw. Then, looking down at his left hand pointing to the shovel, without missing a beat, he said, "And you need a shovel to clean out the chicken shed." Immediately, the left brain, observing the left hand's response without the knowledge of why it had picked that item, put it into a context that would explain it.

In this example, story-making serves to provide a sense of closure and explanation—a way to "make sense" of experience that doesn't quite make sense. It illustrates the way in which people can construct meaning and stories from unrelated elements and the nearness between confabulation and telling a story. Another example of story construction from ambiguous elements is evident in dreams. Edward Pace-Schott, a researcher on the neurobiology of sleep, suggests:

> Dreams create new stories out of nothing. Although dreams contain themes, concerns, dream figures, objects, etc. that correspond closely to waking life, these are only story elements. The story itself weaves these mnemonic items together in a manner far more novel than a simple assemblage or collage, producing an experience having a life-like time frame and life-like (if often bizarre and impossible) causality. (2013, 1)

Thus a dream is not merely a collection of images or felt experience but a complex coordination or integration of disparate elements into a narrative that has some coherence. Dreams have the feeling of cause and effect, some temporal sequencing, setting, and the presence of characters, although their narrative structure is typically more fluid and less organized than consciously directed storytelling.

Yet to say that "dreams create new stories *out of nothing*" is a bit of hyperbole. Common experience would suggest that the elements of our dreams, at least many of them, are familiar to us in some way and we have story-like associations to them. Memory has a powerful role in both dream and story construction so that we pull in feelings, sensory experiences, situations, settings, people, media, and other components that are encoded in memory. However, novel experiences and unfamiliar constructions of life are difficult to encode and retrieve so they end up being simplified and distorted to fit the Procrustean bed of our own consciousness. Bartlett (1932) performed a series of studies looking at memory for stories. He had participants from Cambridge, England, read a short North American folktale taken from native people of the Pacific Northwest. The tale itself does not conform to traditional English-language construction, contains less familiar elements, and might be considered somewhat dreamlike in its minimal explanation of events and temporal sequence. What Bartlett found consistently was that in recalling the tale, his participants made it into something more familiar, so "canoes" might be recalled as "boats," or instead of going "seal-hunting," the men were going "fishing." The stories were rendered into something that conformed to the participants' preexisting conception of the world, resulting in simplified, distorted stories with altered structure and meaning and little detail.

Bartlett used the term *schemata* to describe the many underlying principles by which we make sense of experience and make it conform to our preexisting view of the world. My grandfather had a simplifying schema in which snakes were dangerous and should be killed. I had a simplifying schema in which snakes were objects of fascination and proximity. What was most striking to me, and I suspect to my grandfather, is that until we had an interaction involving snakes and had a collision of worldviews, we were unaware that we had differing schemata. The decision-making process was automatic, unconscious, and consistent. I certainly had no awareness of constructing this particular schema and no intention of altering it. It presented itself to me as simply "true." Bartlett suggests, on the basis of his story-memory research, that the remembering involved in storytelling is a constructive process—it is made up each time that a complex memory is retrieved. He also argues that consciousness reflects an organism's capacity to "turn around" and reflect on its own schemata, rather than just being reflexively determined by them.

It is mind-boggling to consider the many interrelated patterns that we hold as schemata in order to simplify the complexity of living in the world. From attitudes about ourselves, sensory experiences (e.g., foods, scents, etc.), people who are loved, people who are feared, social and political ideas—these are all the "sound bites" of our minds that we listen to but have little awareness of. Certainly marketing forces prey on these perceptions, for example, so something like "organic produce" is transformed into a simplifying schema that may be generally coded as "good" or "desirable," although some people may code it as "too expensive" or "sucker marketing," with very little knowledge of the actual practices that it took to grow, or of "organic" pesticides that can be lethally toxic to bees and neurologically damaging to humans.

In a book of popular psychology exploring love, Hendrix (2007) speculates how some of these schemata play out in intimate relationships. For example, he notes that the distinction of friend versus foe is basic to many living creatures and essential to their adaptation and survival. Turkeys, for example, can distinguish a flying hawk from another soaring bird, or a poisonous from a nonpoisonous snake, and even have a vocabulary to communicate these observations to each other (Hutto, 2011). Hendrix artfully argues that although our brains have much greater complexity, we sometimes make these friend–foe distinctions automatically and end up in situations where we are treating a partner in an intimate relationship as if they were an "enemy," because some schema has been triggered and we move to an experience of threat within our bodies. Only when we are aware that this has happened and begin to explore and share what the schema is does the experience begin to make sense to a puzzled (and irritated) partner.

The writer Chimamanda Adichie (2009) has articulated the danger of a dominant story in the context of culture, class, and race and has provided a moving account of her own difficult encounters with a "single story," both being subjected to it and recognizing it in her own perceptions of the world. She tells the story of growing up on a university campus in east Nigeria. Her mother would encourage her to finish her food, reminding her that their domestic servant's family was very poor, and they would send food and clothing to them to help out. Then while visiting this servant's family in their village, Adichie was startled to see a beautiful basket that the young man's mother had made. Later, as she reflected on that experience, Adichie realized that she had a single story of a life consisting of hunger and poverty for the servant's family, but not artistic skill and beautiful objects.

When Adichie came to the United States to attend college she had a roommate who wondered how she learned to speak English so well, wanted to hear her "tribal" music, and was surprised that Adichie knew how to use a stove. The roommate did not recognize that English is the national language of Nigeria, that Adichie grew up listening to popular music, and that she had a home with comforts that were very similar to those found in the United States. In describing this encounter, Adichie explains, "My roommate had a single story of Africa; a single story of catastrophe. In this single story there was no possibility of Africans being similar to her in any way, no possibility of feelings more complex than pity, no possibility of connection as human equals." Dominant single stories have the potential to reify stereotypes and power structures, preventing genuine encounters of discovery and connection.

Many psychologists have written popular accounts of the research literature related to implicit judgments, biases, and intuitive decision-making, including Kahneman (2011), Banaji and Greenwald (2013), and Gladwell (2007). People are often ready to acknowledge that they have prejudice and biases in their social perceptions and judgments, but that does not always make them easy to recognize or to change. In constructing stories, we are drawing on memories that tend to be encoded and structured in terms of our existing schemata. Yet, we also have the potential to plumb the depths of experience more deeply and carefully to restructure our schemata in new and complicated ways.

Some schemata are likely the combination of "bottom-up" and "top-down" cognition; "bottom-up" relating to the more evolutionarily primitive triggering of fear networks present in lizards and birds, for example, and "top-down" relating to learning, memory, and experience that influences a response. For example, my grandfather's fear of snakes likely represents some primal triggering of a deeply embedded fear response (bottom-up) that LoBue (2013), a psychologist studying cognitive development, has argued is an adaptation for learning that is evolutionary-privileged in mammals. This, combined with the fact that Grampa likely linked information about dangerous snakes, perhaps experiences of snakes, and stories from others about snakes, which reflect the more conscious, "top-down" thinking, probably influenced his reactions.

It is important to note the role of dominant culture in enforcing single stories of consumerism, racism, stereotypical thinking, sexism, gender bias, beauty myths, fear of difference, and myriad other perspectives that become incorporated into our schemata. In reflecting on a particular response pattern it is difficult to determine the extent to which it is "top-down" or "bottom-up"; culturally related "top-down" biases are often perceived as "bottom-up" and may be influenced in both directions (e.g., Kubota, Banaji, and Phelps, 2013).

## How Can Dominant Stories Change?

In considering how to construct new stories for social change that help us out of our ruts, individually and socially, there are several approaches to consider. Conscious awareness of our schemata is certainly part of this process. One way that this can happen is by authentically encountering others who have different perspectives, opinions, and ideas. But this is likely most effective when there is a holding relationship, at least a mutual respect and honesty in the exchange. McGilchrist (2010) provides a compelling revision to considering "left" and "right" hemisphere distinctions. He suggests that the left hemisphere is concerned with technology and manipulation of the world and things in the world, while the right hemisphere is concerned with an embodied interconnected world, in which we are oriented toward the living rather than the mechanical. In his video lecture, *The Divided Brain and the Making of the Western World*, McGilchrist explains:

> Let me make it clear: For imagination you need *both* hemispheres; let me make it very clear: For reason you need *both* hemispheres. So if I had to sum it up I'd say the world of the left hemisphere, dependent on denotative language and abstraction, yields clarity and power to manipulate things that are known, fixed, static, isolated, decontextualized, explicit, general in nature, but ultimately lifeless.
>
> The right hemisphere by contrast yields a world of individual, changing, evolving, interconnected, implicit, incarnate, living beings in the context of the lived world, but in the nature of things never fully graspable, never perfectly known.

McGilchrist argues that the left-hemispheric world has become increasingly dominant so that those means of problem-solving and technology have been employed to try to resolve certain kinds of problems, while fundamentally leaving us stuck in other ways. Extending his thought, I would suggest that only by also engaging the embodied world, through story and relationship, do we have the potential to shift our fundamental schemata rather than just express new iterations of them.

Schemata can be malleable. One good example of this comes from nineteenth-century scientist Francis Galton, who experimented with the schema of paranoia. He decided to start his day by imbuing everything and everyone he met with evil intent. He found that he had to discontinue his experiment early on because he found himself convinced that a horse had malicious intent and realized that he was having difficulty shifting this position (Watson, 1971). It is interesting to speculate that his experiment involved both relational and denotative components, that is, there was both a concrete explicit thought (*others are out to cause me harm*) and a feeling of relational threat.

Hirsh, Mar, and Peterson (2013) argue that personal narratives represent the highest level of integrative thought because they are able to include a great deal of information in compressed form, offer explanations of causal relationships, include emotional context, maintain a sense of identity, and use an empathic perspective of the theory of mind to construe the intentions of others. Cozolino (2003) explains how the brain/body integrates meaning and emotion through the use of stories:

> Storytelling also invokes participation of the body as we gesture or act out the events we are describing. As such, narratives are a valuable tool in the organization and integration of neural networks throughout the nervous system. Memories are distributed throughout the brain and body and are subject to modification. Because we can write and rewrite the stories of ourselves, new stories hold the potential for new ways of experiencing ourselves and our lives. In editing our narratives, we change the organization and nature of our memories and, hence, reorganize our brains as well as our minds. This is a central endeavor in many forms of psychotherapy. (103)

Intriguing research has demonstrated that even sustained reading of a novel, participating deeply in someone else's story, has the potential to change neural connectivity, particularly in areas of the brain that are associated with perspective-taking and story comprehension (Berns, Blaine, Prietula, and Pye 2013). It is valuable to consider both the nature of stories that we tell ourselves and the stories that we tell to others. They have the potential to move us and others beyond the dominant single stories that seek to determine our experience.

## Seeing Snakes in New Ways

I remember two other moments that my grandfather and I shared with respect to snakes. He had brought me fishing along a broad slow stretch of the Charles River in the suburbs of Boston. He didn't fish himself because he didn't want to pay for the license, but he knew the law allowed me to have two fishing poles without a license. Two other men sitting in their lawn chairs had caught a huge catfish. They didn't want to keep it, but my grandfather wanted to bring it home to eat. He went off to his boxy 1964 International Scout to see if he could find a bucket. I had not had a lot of luck fishing, and this fish that I was trying to hold by the tail was impressive. It was also heavy and my grip was slipping. My child-mind suggested that if those guys had caught this fish, then I could too, and that would be more fun than eating it. When no one was looking, with a final little swing, I heaved it down the muddy bank where two quick flips brought it back into the water. My grandfather returned with a bucket a few minutes later, chagrined to find the fish gone. I at least owned up to my motivation, which caused him to sigh, shake his head, and wipe his forehead. It was a sad moment, but one not untinged with a certain appreciation for the nuances of my motivation.

As we were packing up our things to go, I spied a tiny colorful, ringed snake in the grass, and I immediately went to catch it in my hands. My grandfather barked at me not to touch it, and I could hear the genuine fear in his voice. I stopped, not because I was afraid of the snake—I knew it was harmless even though I didn't know exactly what it was—but because I could feel his raw emotion of fear and love, his deep story. Again he saw the disappointment in my face, but we just headed home without talking too much.

I suppose I continued to talk about hog-nosed snakes and tried to educate him on the subject. The following summer, on a hot day, I was in the basement playing with my electric slot cars when I heard my grandfather at the back door shouting, "Where's Jimmy?" He looked slightly shaken and was breathless. He said he had found a "puff adder" and instead of killing it had thrown some dirt on it and put a box over it. He encouraged me to go up with my older brother and see it. I was elated. We ran up, found the box, tilted it back, but the snake was long gone. I realized in that moment that both my grandfather and I had constructed richer, more complicated stories of our relationship to snakes that came from our love and admiration for each other. I developed a greater respect for "wild" things and my potential to harm them, so I don't pick up snakes anymore, even if I am not afraid of them.

Narratives are a crucial way in which we organize ourselves in relation to the world, personally and culturally. Appreciating the ways in which our underlying schemas can limit us and keep us stuck provides a strategy for fundamentally shifting the stories we tell and the stories we live. Generalization, rationalization, and abstraction distance us from felt experience and reinforce dominant single stories based on these schemata. Acknowledging our ignorance, focusing on our conscious awareness of felt experience, keeping good notes in the moment, embracing diverse encounters, and acknowledging our own rut of the single story has the potential to allow us to tell more complex, embodied, ambiguous, and authentic stories. I still have never seen a hog-nosed snake in the wild.

## References

Adichie, Chimamnda Ngozi. 2009. The danger of a single story. *TED Talks video.* http://www.ted.com/talks/chimamanda_adichie_the_danger_of_a_single_story .html (accessed March 2014).

Banaji, Mahzarin, and Anthony Greenwald. 2013. *Blindspot: Hidden biases of good people.* New York: Random House.

Bartlett, Frederic. 1932. *Remembering.* London: Oxford University Press.

Berns, Gregory S., Kristina Blaine, Michael J. Prietula, and Brandon E. Pye. 2013. Short- and long-term effects of a novel on connectivity in the brain. *Brain Connectivity,* 3:590–600.

Cozolino, Louis. 2003. *The neuroscience of psychotherapy: Building and rebuilding the human brain.* New York: Norton.

Gazzaniga, Michael. 2005. *The ethical brain.* New York: Dana.

———. 2012. The "interpreter" in your head spins stories to make sense of the world. *Discover Magazine,* August 1. http://discovermagazine.com/2012/brain/22 -interpreter-in-your-head-spins-stories (accessed March 2014).

Gladwell, Malcolm. 2007. *Blink: The power of thinking without thinking.* New York: Back Bay.

Hendrix, Harville. 2007. *Getting the love you want.* New York: Henry Holt.

Hirsh, J. B., R. A. Mar, and J. B. Peterson. 2013. Personal narratives as the highest level of cognitive integration. *The Behavioral and Brain Sciences,* 36:216–17.

Hutto, Joe. 2011. *Illumination in the flatwoods: A season living among the wild turkey.* Guilford, CT: Lyons.

Kahneman, Daniel. 2011. *Thinking, fast and slow.* New York: Farrar, Straus and Giroux.

Kubota, Jennifer T., Mahzarin R. Banaji, and Elizabeth A. Phelps. 2012. The neuroscience of race. *Nature Neuroscience*, 15:940–48.

LoBue, Vanessa. 2013. What are we so afraid of? How early attention shapes our most common fears. *Child Development Perspectives*, 7:38–42.

McGilchrist, Iain. 2010. *The divided brain and the making of the Western world.* RSA video, 32:11. http://www.east-west-dichotomy.com/iain-mcgilchrist-the-divided-brain-the-making-of-the-western-world-full-lecture-text (accessed March 2014).

Pace-Schott, Edward. 2013. Dreaming as a story-telling instinct. *Frontiers in Psychology*, 4(159):1–4. http://www.ncbi.nlm.nih.gov/pmc/articles/PMC3613603/pdf/fpsyg-04-00159.pdf (accessed March 2014).

Snedigar, Robert. 1963. *Our small native animals: Their habits and care.* New York: Dover.

Watson, Irving. 1971. *The great psychologists.* New York: Lippincott.

## *Snapshot*

**Sherry Reiter, Brooklyn, New York**

*Poetry therapy pioneer, educator, clinical social worker, writer, storyteller*

Words are the umbilical cords through which we seek nurturance, humor, and comfort from others. Without words, each of us remains alone with our own thoughts. No feedback, no dialogue, and very often stuck in the cacophony of our own thoughts. Connection to others remains a source of vitality, energy, joy. When pain is shared, words have the ability to transmute and transform suffering.

For more than three decades, I have worked with individuals and writing circles (called "poetry therapy" in therapeutic settings). I have helped professionals to use the written and spoken word to assist people to find their unique voice. The Creative Righting Center is a center of training for persons who want to learn creative methods for personal transformation. Note that the term "righting" suggests an innate self-righting or balancing process when the curves of life throw us off balance.

I was privileged to create with my talented students Poets-Behind-Bars, a project of the center for maximum-security prisoners in the Indiana State Prison. Twelve volunteers are matched with twelve inmates to write to each other through e-mail. As one inmate/poet said, "I felt there was one person in this world that wanted to hear what I had to say."

As a counselor and trainer of poetry therapy, I have heard many astonishing stories.

In 2009, my book *Writing Away the Demons: Stories of Creative Coping through Transformative Writing* (North Star) was published. In it are the stories of thirteen individuals who wrote their way through crisis to psychological survival. These stories are precious because they represent the soul-work of words; the writings are like maps showing where people have been and where they are going.

What I love best about word work is that it makes the world a little bit larger—and a little bit smaller because it brings people together. It is not only work of the mind but of heart and of soul. It is powerful enough to pierce the walls that exist—whether in a prison or our own minds.

www.thecreativerightingcenter.com

# *Snapshot*

## Seema Reza, Bethesda, Maryland

*Recreational arts program coordinator at military hospitals, poet, and writer*

In the past three years I have learned more about suffering than I did in the last thirty years. I began working with service members returning from combat, listening to and helping them express their stories, first at an Army Medical Center's Arts and Crafts Center and later building innovative programming at two military hospitals in the Washington, DC, area.

During the same time, I made the decision to finally end a dysfunctional marriage, lost my father suddenly, transitioned to partial custody of my two children, and began to navigate life on my own in a way I never had. These have also been some of the most professionally and creatively fulfilling, integrated, productive years. I completed a BFA in creative writing and wrote *When the World Breaks Open*, a mixed-genre book of poetry and prose forthcoming from Red Hen Press. With the support of multiple hospital departments, I conceived of and implemented a recreational arts program in two military treatment facilities in the National Capital Region.

The military recreational arts program was developed to include unique and existing community weeklong workshops that blend arts modalities and a curriculum of writing prompts with the input of supervising clinicians. Through the program, veterans have become published writers and visual artists. Most importantly, they have learned to use their stories as a way to connect to other people rather than isolate themselves. Between 2011 and 2013, with the help of colleagues, volunteers, and visiting artists, the activities I coordinated went from serving about 130 participants monthly to serving nearly 500 each month.

These have been scary years. Everything I believed necessary to my survival seemed to disappear or shift. I began a search for new answers, and in my search I have come to accept the search itself as a way of life. I have discovered open doors in places where even the hinges were hidden and unlikely sources of wisdom because I was willing to listen to things I may have dismissed at another time. I found relevant books by reviews in magazines that I opened at doctors' offices, leads from coworkers, articles in newspapers left on the seat of the MTA car on my commute to work, and new perspectives from strangers. Each of these exposures has guided how I use personal narrative as a tool to heal the mind, the relationship between the audience and written work, the role of the artist and, in particular, the teaching artist, in society.

I love most of all witnessing the relationship between participants as they help each other move forward. Writing can be an isolating endeavor. We sit with the page, immersed in our thoughts and experiences, uncertain if our voices are valuable or valid. When we share our work—either through public readings and exhibits or in a workshop setting—we begin to feel a sense of responsibility to contribute to the collective narrative of our time.

www.seemareza.com

2

# "Everyone's Life Is a Book"

## *Public Housing Women Write for Their Lives*

CARYN MIRRIAM-GOLDBERG

Newborn Elara sleeps on her Navajo cradleboard while I hold newborn Jafiya, who stares at me with shining eyes. Both Elara's mother, Melanie K. Jones from the Navajo nation, and Jafiya's mom, Juliana Birdling from Nigeria, are part of "A Circle of Women, a Circle of Words," a weekly writing workshop I facilitated at a Kansas housing authority. Melanie's and Juliana's other children are in a childcare center across the street, and we just finished lasagna, salad, and brownies before I ask the women to write about their greatest dreams for themselves.

The resident services office of the Lawrence-Douglas County Housing Authority made the workshop possible from 2000 to 2010, providing childcare, dinner, the meeting room, my fee, and new journals and pens for each six-week session. Started with a small grant from the National Association for Poetry Therapy Foundation, the workshop was so successful that Kris Hermanson, the visionary director of the resident services office, found continued funding through Department of Housing and Urban Development grants. She explains, "The grants that support public housing tenants imply that if you're poor, you're a bad parent. If you're poor, you're not educated. If you're poor, you have some deficiency in some way as opposed to it being a life situation. I wanted to offer classes that allowed people to explore their life circumstances in a way that wasn't judgmental, that could bring people together in a positive way" (Hermanson, 2014).

The workshop also brought public housing residents the kind of enrichment usually unavailable to low-income people. Marilyn Thunderhawk, a longtime workshop participant, says, "The workshop was different and wonderful for a lower-income person who never has an opportunity like this. It was rare opportunity" (Thunderhawk, 2014). Pat Schneider, founder of the Amherst Writers and Artists method for community writing groups, started out leading a group for low-income women in a Chicopee, Massachusetts, housing project to provide the same kind of opportunity: "The goal is something that most low-income adults have never experienced in their lives: to be respected as an artist. To have their own voices honored. To have their stories received as important and beautiful. The goal is self-esteem" (2003, 263).

The workshop served single moms who dropped out of high school because of drugs or babies, elders who fell on hard times because of illness or broken marriages, and middle-aged women hanging on by just a thread in the hard winds of mental or physical illness. The women circled around the table came from the Navajo, Arikara, and Lakota nations; from Nigerian towns or Mississippi slums; or from too many long stays in juvenile detention, jail, or mental hospitals. All of them knew what it was to live at the most extreme margins of our country, and they found unity and understanding in one another's writing.

## From Edgewood's Edge to the Commons: The Workshop

Once every season, we began a six-week session in Edgewood, a large maze of ground-level apartments that was part of the 369 public housing units in Lawrence. Meeting Tuesdays from 6:30–8:30 p.m. gave us enough time for visiting over dinner while I first reviewed the ground rules and explained the first writing prompt before giving the women ten to fifteen minutes to write.

The ground rules took the pressure off the women and helped them avoid censoring or demeaning themselves, particularly for not having finished college, high school, or even elementary school. I told them not to worry about spelling, grammar, or making sense. "When you write in your own voice and tell your stories, the writing will be strong," I regularly reminded them. No one needed to read aloud, or follow the suggested writing prompt, and the only thing not allowed was self-deprecation before they read their work. "I know most of us have the urge to say, 'I can read this, but it's stupid and not as good as everyone else's writing.' You don't need to reinforce that message in your head," I told them weekly. They nodded in understanding.

Often I brought in poems chosen for their tilt toward hope and accessibility, drawn from writers such as Rumi, Mary Oliver, Ursula LeGuin, David Waggoner, and David Whyte, or more ancient writers. We would read a poem aloud, sometimes twice, and that in itself was important for some of the women, who struggled with literacy and public speaking.

Sometimes we passed around my basket of antique postcards, the women drawing out three or four that appealed to them. "Choose one postcard of a setting, another of a magic object that helps you achieve something you want in life, and a third postcard with a person or animal who helps you," I might suggest. I also brought in a basket with small objects—stones, plastic animals, feathers, marbles, whatever little trinkets I found around my house or among my kids' unused toys—and had the women draw out random objects and then incorporate them into a story or poem. Sometimes we used sentence stems, in which writers fill in the blanks, repeating the sentence stem to add more dimensions, such as "I used to be ___ but now I'm ___." Such an exercise, as Melanie wrote about, helped the writers name themselves on their own terms:

**I Used to Be**

I used to be a spirit
but now I'm just human.
I used to be a daughter
but now I'm a mother.
I used to be a wild child
but now I'm a mentor.
I used to be a student
but now I'm a teacher.
I used to be vicious
but now I'm gentle.

I used to be a heartbreaker
but now I'm married.
I used to be a good friend
but now I'm an acquaintance.
I used to be a runner
but now I'm a walker.
I used to be imaginative
but now I'm serious.
I used to be tough
but now I'm just rough.
I used to be gorgeous
but now I'm beautiful.
I used to be a girl
but now I'm a woman.

(Mirriam-Goldberg, 2006, 23)

The group was diverse: "They saw themselves as neighbors, as women, not that they didn't notice their different ethnicity," says Kris (Hermanson, 2014). Through writing, they educated each other and me about the visceral effects of racism, chronic illness, and mental illness. The Native American women wrote about how they had been forcibly removed or surrendered for a time by their families to attend boarding schools bent on beating their native traditions, language, and memories out of them. Some, like Ella Farmer, an older African American woman, dropped out of school in third grade to help her family in the cotton fields of the Deep South. Others, like "Mickey,"[1] a startlingly brilliant writer with a substantial intellect, balanced life as a schizophrenic with expansive loves—Mickey's for guinea pigs and poetry.

Writing gave the women common ground to share their similar and different challenges, if not always the strength to overcome such challenges. "Writing makes your challenges real, allows you to process them, and allows you not to necessarily to break free but perhaps move forward. I hope they took away a better understanding of their strength, resiliency and the possibilities that are available to them," Kris explains (Hermanson, 2014).

What circumstances brought the women into "the system" of public support had also diminished the strength and resiliency born of good self-esteem and success. Yet when it comes to how they landed in the economic tar pits of our culture, the answers are complicated and overlapping. "The world's most ruthless killer and the greatest cause of suffering on earth . . . is extreme poverty," states a report by the World Health Organization (WHO, 1995, 1). Research worldwide has continually confirmed that poverty increases the risk of addiction, abuse, physical and mental illness, and limited access to education, risks that altogether multiply the others' dangerous effects. Eric Turkheimer, a psychology professor who studied complex human traits, explains, "No complex behaviors in free-ranging humans are caused by a linear and additive set of causes" (2006, 104). For the women in the workshop, these causes included parents and grandparents in poverty, inadequate education and job training, limited economic opportunities, living in communities where drugs and alcohol were widely used for self-medication, family and institutional abuse, learning differences, chronic illness, and the effects of racism and oppression on livelihood, housing, education, and self-esteem. Altogether, these overlapping factors can lead to what Turkheimer called the "Gloomy Prospect," an insidious and overwhelming perspective that limits expectations and opportunities for low-income people.

Despite a lifetime of being told they had gloomy prospects, the women came together from the edges of their lives to write in the commons: a communal space they composed out of their words. For some, the experience made all the difference in tipping the balance toward a better life. For others, it wasn't enough.

## The Closet of Mental Illness

As a child, Mickey spent hours and even days in the closet, locked up by abusive family members. She was diagnosed with schizophrenia as an adult after years of homelessness followed her childhood of severe abuse and neglect. She had little reason to trust the world beyond her housing authority one-bedroom apartment. "Money is not a guarantor of mental health, nor does its absence necessarily lead to mental illness. However, it is generally conceded that poverty can be both a determinant and a consequence of poor mental health," researchers Langer and Michael wrote in their 1963 study on life stress and mental illness (Murali and Oyebode, 2004).[2] Given that the economic divides have only widened and health-care costs have multiplied over the last five decades, we can easily make the case for the increased link between poverty and mental illness.[3]

Likewise, activities that help people dissolve some of their life stress can improve health (Murali and Oyebode, 2004), and this was the case for Mickey, a white woman in her mid-forties. The writing workshop was the first activity she participated in at the housing authority, and after her first session, only wild horses or the housing authority staff, when Mickey was having a bad day (mostly related to not taking her medication), could keep her from coming back. She would get ready for the workshop several hours ahead of time and was often at the door an hour early, clutching her notebook to her chest, pacing, and smoking a cigarette. Participating in the workshop also dissolved enough barriers for her that she began showing up regularly at the resident services office to use the computers or visit with staff.

The workshop was one of the only places Mickey could shine. A gifted poet, she came up with delicate and precise images and found the rhythm in strong and compelling poems. In one poem, she wrote about the delicate beauty and scent of lily-of-the-valley and how lying down next to such flowers would allow her to lower the volume of her fears, which often ruled her life. Her work was excellent enough to have gotten her into any number of creative writing programs and literary journals, but her life didn't allow for even dreaming in such directions.

Interacting with the group helped Mickey see she was neither alone nor some psychological anomaly. In studying the effect poetry therapy had on schizophrenic patients, Edgar, Hazley, and Levitt (1985) write about several patients who couldn't articulate their problems until they looked into the mirror of someone else's poem and saw their own emotions reflected. "This not only was cathartic but also permitted a sharing of common fears that were secret, personal, and festering until this point. With such objective externalization, they found that others shared their torment, and this brought about a common bond" (186).

Writing also gave workshop participants a way to put into some kind of narrative order the pattern of their lives, something especially important to Mickey, who was duking it out each day with mental illness. In Mazza's study on poetry therapy, he cites the research of Widroe and Davidson, who noted back in 1961 "that writing is especially helpful with schizophrenic clients by providing a vehicle to express order and concreteness in their daily activities" (1999, 12).

Mickey was one of several women with debilitating mental illness. Gloria, a catatonic, would come to class, sit quietly with a glazed but satisfied look on her face, occasionally nod, but never write or talk. I sought consultation from a senior psychotherapist and registered poetry therapist who assured me that Gloria was getting enough out of just being there, and it was best not to push her to participate more. There were also women who suffered from severe depression. When they felt well enough to leave their homes, they easily wrote about the black hole they just climbed out of, but too often they would soon enough vanish from the group again.

Mickey was actively involved in the workshop for at least seven years before the bottom fell out. After her guinea pig accidentally got loose and was killed by local dogs, her paranoia and agitation were dialed large. One outburst led to another, she refused to take her meds or see her therapist, and over a series of months, she lost her apartment and thus her independence. The last I heard, she was living out of state with relatives, who may or may not be some of her past abusers.

Marilyn, reflecting on years of being in the workshop with Mickey, told me: "She had all these years not being homeless, and that's an accomplishment for her [to have housing]. You've got to realize what a triumph that is for her to have done that much" (Thunderhawk, 2014). I hadn't considered such a perspective before, and although I'm glad that Mickey had a home of her own for so many years, I fear that Mickey is locked back in the closet of mental illness. Writing was her lifeline, and wherever she is now, I hope she can still put pen to paper.

## The Mother of All Invention: Low-Income Mothers

Melanie knew she wanted to be a mother from a young age. Raised on and off the Navajo reservation, today she's the mother of six, ranging from newborn to eighteen. As a young mother married to the father of her children, Melanie and her husband were able to save up enough and work together to move to a Habitat for Humanities home in the neighborhood. Melanie's dreams drew her to her traditions as a Navajo woman, and especially to her grandparents in her poetry, often in search of stories to explain the real center of her life. "Everyone needs a creation story," writes Lewis Mehl-Madrona, "just as much as cultures need stories about their origins" (2005, 14).

**The Bobcat's Gift**

Long ago before even you or me lived a great nation.
The people of this nation called themselves, "the people."
They spoke their own languages and brought gifts to one another.
They traveled far and wide to receive great messages from grandfather.
Sometimes these great messages were brought by holy spirits
in the form of animals. These animals would help and guide you
and you would be given a talisman,
and things would be as they should be.

I've been told this from my own beginning.
Sacred songs were sung, smoke would carry these songs
as prayers to our creator.
These things were told before my path was taken.

And here I am seeking joy and love.
Here I am among the falling leaves of autumn
seeking what I am to be.
I love all that has been given to me,
yet I seem to feel something is missing.
I am a person put here alone
but the spirits of the earth, my mother, the lives
she helped create are all around.
I am not a lonely spirit here among the fallen leaves.
It is then I hear footsteps upon the path.
I turn to see my brother, the bobcat, looking at me.
His eyes fill with love, speak this language
from long ago. I have this connection to his spirit.

My brother says, *Here I am. Dry your weeping eyes.*
*Take upon you this single stone to remind you*
*from where you come and also how meaningful you are.*
*You are my sister, just as important to creator*
*as this single stone. Carry it upon you.*
*It is the symbol and answer you seek.*
*It is the love that Grandfather has for you.*
*Great and small, strong and enduring.*
*Love from grandfather is as your love for others.*
*Keep this stone upon you to remember always.*

I hold in my hand this love from grandfather,
and my brother walks away silently among the red
fallen leaves. My heart fills with joy and love.

(Mirriam-Goldberg, 2006, 43)

Melanie's climb out of public housing was the exception to the rule. Many of the other mothers in the group were single or had husbands or boyfriends who were either incarcerated, in recovery, or actively addicted to drugs and/or alcohol or, in at least one case (and likely more), abusive to their partners. According to a recent study by the Brookings Institute, more than 4.1 single-mother families live at or below the poverty level, a number that has been disproportionately increasing over recent years (Yen, 2013). Jacqueline Kirby (n.d.) from Ohio University found that 25 percent of all children are born to single mothers today, and another 40 percent of children born to two parents will experience a family breakup.

It's no surprise that single-mother households were the norm more than the exception in public housing, and over the years, more than half of the women in the workshop were single mothers. Coming to the writing workshop was one of the only activities available to the women in Edgewood that gave them a break from caring for their children, working, or looking for work. This workshop was their oasis, their place to be off duty from 24/7 caregiving, their time to return to the dreams of their girlhood and dream new dreams for their children and themselves.

Such was the case for Flo Laducer, who was thrown out of the house by her Native American parents for getting pregnant by an African American man. Born in North Dakota, Flo grew up in Lawrence with roots off the reservation. But as she explains, "I am and was raised to an Arikara woman. My traditions, my talk, and my mannerisms are all Arika in nature." Her parents were "boarding school Indians," who were ripped away from their families. She says, "They were raised hard and taught that separate is better." After losing the support of her family while seven months' pregnant, she slept outside a few nights and stayed with her boyfriend's mother until she got into public housing at age twenty. "I ended up in the system because my family disliked the father of my child and my child. I was very much isolated and alone. I managed through all the troubles though somehow. Call it God. Call it Creator. Call it love" (Laducer, 2013).

Flo went on to have three children; the first two are half black, half Native American, and the third child is all Native American. Today, her oldest child is in college at age sixteen, working on his AA in math, and she lives in North Dakota, where she works in information technologies for a tribal college, Fort Berthold Community College. She credits the writing workshop with igniting a journey that continues to this day. She writes:

> It's been over ten years since I sat in a room and wrote creatively with other women. Many seasons have passed since my journey to find myself began. It all started in a little red building in a public housing complex and each memory plays through my mind like an old movie reel. It is in that room where I learned to love myself a bit more. It is in that room where my mind expanded beyond my day-to-day living of an impoverished life. Surrounded by women who could see that we needed something to pull us through . . . to pull me through the hard times one is either born into or suffering by circumstance. I learned to see with my eyes in that room that I was someone with potential.
>
> Now one could argue that it was merely a creative writing class and you would be right, but what is teaching creative writing but teaching creative thought? And from imagination springs dreams. I still hear the remarks of how touching my words are but my true love came from those evenings with those women. I have fallen in love with the written word, and because of my love I have been working towards a degree in Lab Science with a year to go. I now own my own home on a little piece of dirt with mountainous views that still stun me

> when my eyes gaze upon them. You can change your whole life if you picture it differently. (Laducer, 2013)

"It basically gives you strength to survive for another week," Beverly Morrison, another single mother who participated in the workshop, says. "It's like a church. I would consider it a religious experience" (Paget, 2003).

## Stranger in a Strange Land

Ella walked into the first class slowly, a little unsure. It took her months before she would meet my eyes, and she often talked so quietly that we could barely hear her read. Raised in the Deep South, she lived in the Midwest now, close to gaggles of grandkids who would flood her house whenever their mothers needed respite. A champion of surviving abusive men, extreme poverty, debilitating depression, racism, and chronic illness, she was subject to mini-strokes and sometimes seemed to be in a world apart. Yet she wrote eloquently of her faith and identity.

One of Ella's closest friendships came out of the group. Marilyn and Ella bonded over writing and quilting, and Marilyn was part of Ella's last year of life, before she died suddenly of a heart attack in 2011. "At Christmas I would take her card over to her, or we would bake cookies, or she would say, 'I'm making this quilt, can you come over and help me?' That was a meaningful friendship we ended up having that we wouldn't have had otherwise" (Thunderhawk, 2014).

Marilyn, a member of the Lakota nation, was born on the Rosebud Indian Reservation in South Dakota. She was one of twelve children in a family that moved often for her father's work, sometimes living on the reservation, sometimes off. Eventually, the whole family moved to Dallas as part of a relocation program that landed Native American people in urban areas to begin new lives.

Marilyn wanted a college degree and to live near the mountains, yet she ended up with neither because of single motherhood and a mysterious debilitating illness. By the time she discovered she had a rare combination of severe low blood sugar and diabetes, and found her way back to health, she was living in public housing, her son was grown, and her prospects for finishing her degree had slipped beyond reach. "I was pretty much on my way to death, but I was meant to go on. That ended up being very spiritual," she says of her survival (Thunderhawk, 2014).

Both Ella and Marilyn never felt Kansas was their true home, but through the arts—writing and quilting—Marilyn makes meaning of the life she has now:

***A Moment of Blessing***

> When I completed my broken star quilt top, an amazing thing began to happen. The outer tips of the star quilt design reminded me of mountain tops. An excitement began inside of me and grew and grew until I could hardly sit still to complete the last stitches for the quilt top. I couldn't understand it because I was so thrilled that it became beyond belief. This was only a quilt top after all.
>
> Soon I was in a state of complete euphoria. I was on cloud nine, and I stayed there for an entire week! I never experienced this kind of mountain top experience.
>
> Later on, I figured that it was a dream come true, and the dream lay dormant in my heart until I got the broken star done.
>
> The heart has so many mysteries. Who can fathom what the heart has to show us? In a life in which so many dreams never came true, this experience showed me that your own heart has so many hidden treasures, that not to seek them is probably the worst betrayal that a person inflicts on themselves.
>
> "To thine own self be true" has taken on a whole new meaning since last spring.
>
> (Mirriam-Goldberg, 2006, 85)

Looking at her true self, Marilyn found "someone who loves learning." She also affirmed her own narrative, not of dying or just hanging on, but living artfully with meaning.

Juliana Birdling was also a stranger in a strange land. She left nursing school in Nigeria in 1984 to be with her Nigerian immigrant husband and raise a family in the Midwest. In addition to Jafiya, who is now ten years old, Juliana has three more children, the oldest twenty-eight. Juliana and her family first settled in Missouri, but after her husband finished his degree and worked a number of years, the family moved to Lawrence so he could pursue graduate study at the University of Kansas. With Juliana working at home caring for her four children, and her husband a full-time student, the family qualified for public housing.

Juliana found inspiration and encouragement, especially as a non-native speaker, in the workshop. "Everyone writes whatever naturally comes to them, and for me, it was all about writing the story in my mind. By listening to whatever people write, you learn a lot about who they are" (Birdling, 2014). Although Juliana wants to pick up where she left off in her education to be a nurse, she must now wait until her husband, who just finished his doctorate, finds work. Ten years ago, with Jafiya as a newborn, that wait was almost too long to ponder. Yet the workshop gave Juliana a way to continue learning and make clear to herself and others her future goals, as she writes about in this poem:

**Any Learning Never Ends**

Our learning never ends, which brings me back
to my future goals in life that are to go to school,
to never say you are too old to go to school.
You are never too old to go to school.

I would like to go to school to study something
that will help or heal someone enough.
That's satisfaction to me. That is why
I would like to be a nurse in the future
so that I will work at any hospital
to help the ones in need.

Pray for the best, to be here when needed
and the rest be done by somebody higher than you.
Do your best or let demands move your caring
toward what needs to be done.
It seems like the more they grow,
the more our help needs to go forth.

You learn to be patient, helpful, caring,
and you can never get it all. You think you get it

but sometimes you end up with nothing.
But it's never an end—you can learn
and learning never ends.

(Mirriam-Goldberg, 2006, 59)

Writing in community can't necessarily make a person's dreams come true, but it can and does help women like Ella, Marilyn, and Juliana remember those dreams. Learning to share with others such dreams, and witness their own, was central to what we did together in the workshop. Being witnessed helped the women feel the true weight of their words, and what they believed, needed, were ready for most at this point in their lives. In one of his dozens of studies, James W. Pennebaker, the foremost researcher on the connection between writing and health, concluded:

> Writing forces people to stop and reevaluate their life circumstance. The mere act of writing also demands a certain degree of structure as well as the basic labeling or acknowledging of their emotions. A particularly rich feature of the process is that these inchoate emotions and emotional experiences are translated into words. This analog-to-digital process demands a different representation of the events in the brain, in memory, and in the ways people think on a daily basis. (Pennebaker and Chang, 2011, 436)

In turn, as the women learned to listen to themselves without judgment, they discovered how to offer the same to others within and beyond the workshop. Marilyn explains, "Over time, I made that discovery that people want to be listened to so much." Pennebaker agrees, explaining how his research shows that through expressive writing, people tend to "talk more; they connect with others differently. They are now better able to take advantage of social support. And with these cognitive and social changes, many of their unhealthy behaviors abate" (436).

Pennebaker also tells us that such writing isn't a panacea for everything, and when it works, for whom it works, and how it works still needs further research. Yet he's talking here about expressive writing as part of a contained study rather than as a way for people to make community. The added benefit of sharing deeply in a group helped women, who would too often not be visible in the community, share their truths with each other and others, and discover how much they deserve to put their stories, questions, and perspectives out into the world.

## Through the Cracks: Addiction, Recovery, and Relapse

"Lana,"[4] an exotic dancer in recovery from drug addiction, came to the workshop ready to begin her life anew. Although she had lost her three children because of her previous jail time resulting from a crack addiction, she had made so much progress after rehab that now she had her children back with her, and they all lived in a housing authority unit with Lana's new boyfriend, a man with a steady job who took well to the kids. Lana ended her reign as "Frost" at a local topless club so she could work a minimum-wage job at a local grocery store, getting paid a fraction of her exotic dancing income but distancing herself from the drug temptations born of a late-night club lifestyle. She had just passed her GED and was planning to start classes at a community college as soon as her youngest started school in a few months.

Lana was a gifted writer and loving presence in the group, always able to see the best in what her fellow participants were writing. Her comments on their work were particularly and consistently insightful. One evening, Mickey read a somewhat disjointed piece of writing about love for her first guinea pig, who had recently died, and how the government was engaging in mind-control experiments, finishing it while trembling a little from her shakiness on her new meds. Lana leaned over to her and said, "I hear you that you miss your guinea pig. I know that ache." Then she smiled her Julia Roberts' smile, touched the top of Mickey's hand, and nodded. Mickey smiled back.

In fact, Lana was so impressive as a writer and supportive member of the community that I talked with Housing Authority Resident Services staff about creating a program to train her to facilitate groups like this one as part of how she could make her living. With a little help, she could begin taking classes at a local community college, something she was interested in, and earn a degree to add to her street smarts.

After eighteen months of talking with Lana before and after classes regularly about how well she was doing, how hard it was to believe in herself, and how big her dreams were for a woman who had done time—she wanted a full-time job as a teacher, her own home, and for her children to get to go camping once in a while—Lana vanished. She didn't show up for group one autumn night, and no one had any idea where she was. Within a few days, the sharp news landed: Lana had started using crack again with her boyfriend. Both were caught by the police in a grocery store parking lot. Lana was thrown in jail, her children were taken into the foster care system with no hope of her ever recovering them again, and after numerous hearings, she was sentenced to a long jail sentence.

I still mourn for Lana and the others like her who were close to pulling themselves out of the gravitational pull of addiction. Such a relapse is not unusual. According to a study on people like Lana, who suffer from both addiction and mental illness, one third of people recovering from crack cocaine addictions relapse within a year, and almost 100 percent have an incident of relapse within a decade. For people like Lana, who surely suffered from addiction and may or may not have had mental illness complications, one incident was all it took to set into motion the end of all her plans and dreams (Xie, McHugo, Fox, and Drake , 2005, 1).

Did the workshop make a difference in Lana's life? Kris speculates, "At some point in her life, maybe she'll remember that moment [the writing workshop] and go back to that point in the Slinky. I mean, we're focused on outcome, and sometimes the process is enough. Sometimes just the opportunity to even dip your toe in the water is enough. Would any of them have done that on their own? Written about their lives or even thought about it on their own? Maybe now they do" (Hermanson, 2014).

## The Publication Party for "A Circle of Women, A Circle of Words"

The circle around the table turned into a crescent of women on stage facing an audience of more than 200 people at the Lawrence Arts Center on September 12, 2006. Our anthology, *A Circle of Women, a Circle of Words*, was just published jointly by the housing authority and Mammoth Publications. None of us on stage, because of the lighting, could see the audience, but we heard their laughter and felt their attention as they listened. Mickey, in a suit jacket, dress pants, and a silk shirt, couldn't stop smiling. Juliana wrapped herself and her considerable hair in purple African cloth from her Nigerian homeland. Ella wore her best church dress, and while she looked down as she read, she kept grinning. Marilyn took the microphone with ease when it was her turn, stood up, and read:

> My heart takes up its task again when I open my eyes in the morning from yet another series of dreams my consciousness is left to decipher from my screaming unconscious mind. I don't like it when my minds get in the way of my melting heart, my joyful heart, my struggling to grasp the deeper meaning heart, my bleeding heart, and oh my brave strong heart so wanting to cover us all. I once read this little saying at the beginning of a biography, "What is the use of talking when there is no end of talking because there is no end of things in the heart?" (Mirriam-Goldberg, 2006, 5)

This was one of the first and only times in our community that low-income women of public housing had their say. The mostly middle-class audience, including city commissioners and various movers and shakers of our town, mingled easily with the expansive friends and family of the women. Juliana brought everyone she's related to, and other women, almost everyone they knew.

After the reading, the women waited in a line with me to shake hands and sign books. "It's like a wedding," I whispered to them.

> "It's better than my wedding," one of the women told me.
>
> "It's the best night of my life," says another, then another, and another.

"Everyone was feeling such a sense of accomplishment," Kris remembers. "I think of Ella, who felt invisible 99 percent of the time, on stage reading her own works, and how she would have never thought that was possible. That support from the public—those faces in the audience of people who could potentially be judgmental against them and stigmatize them—was huge. The women shared pretty intimate stuff, and they had the courage to do that. The reception was so empowering for all of them, and ultimately healing" (Hermanson, 2014).

I passed on the workshop facilitation to writer and teacher Laurie Martin-Frydman in 2008, and the workshop ended in 2010 for lack of funding, but its effect carries on. The women I interviewed for this piece all spoke of the workshop as a touchstone in their lives, something they would think about when they needed to remember their strength and vision. Whether or not they're still writing, free or imprisoned in one way or another, as Marilyn reminds us, "Everyone has a contribution to make. Everyone's life is a book" (Thunderhawk, 2013).

## Notes

1. "Mickey's" name is a pseudonym, and identifying details have been changed.

2. Langer and Michael's study on this connection, called the Midtown Manhattan Study, followed the New Haven study by Hollingshead and Redlich in 1958, both of which found "a direct relationship between the experience of poverty and a high rate of emotional disturbance, as well as differential availability and use of treatment modes and facilities by different social classes. Many assume that the socio-economic class gradient with respect to disease can mostly be explained by differences in health care access" (Murali and Oyebode, 2004).

3. According to Jack Carney, "Ultimately, there are no discrete data that clearly enumerate the persons who are poor and have a presumed serious mental illness. While it is undoubtedly substantial, the precise number appears highly variable, ranging from as few as 2.7 million persons to as many as 15 million. This wide variability should not be surprising since many folks eligible for governmental social welfare benefits often don't apply for them, and the public mental health system itself is a porous system, with service recipients moving in and out of it in haphazard fashion. It's also indicative of how little attention has been paid to poverty as a causative agent of presumed serious mental illness that the scope of the problem, the number of persons affected, is so uncertain" (2012).

4. "Lana" cannot be reached. Her name is a pseudonym, and identifying details have been altered.

## References

Birdling, Juliana. Discussion with the author. January 2014.

Carney, Jack. 2012. Poverty and mental illness: You can't have one without the other. In *Mad in America: Science, Psychiatry and Community*. http://www.madinamerica.com/2012/03/poverty-mental-illness-you-cant-have-one-without-the-other/ (accessed January 23, 2014).

Edgar, Kenneth F., Richard Hazley, and Herbert I. Levitt. 1985. Poetry therapy with hospitalized schizophrenics. In *Poetry as healer: Mending the troubled mind*, ed. Jack J. Leedy, 184–92. New York: Vanguard.

Hermanson, Kris. Discussion with author. January 2014.

Kirby, Janet. n.d. The effects of single parenting on the family. http://www3.uakron.edu/schulze/401/readings/singleparfam.htm (accessed January 2013).

Laducer, Flo. Private communication. December 10, 2013.

Mazza, Nicholas. 1999. *Poetry therapy: Interface of the arts and psychology*. Boca Raton, FL: CRC Press.

Mehl-Madrona, Lewis. 2005. *Coyote wisdom: The power of story of healing*. Rochester, VT: Bear & Co.

Mirriam-Goldberg, Caryn, ed. 2006. *A circle of women, a circle of words*. Lawrence, KS: Lawrence-Douglas County Housing Authority and Mammoth Publications.

Murali, Vijaya, and Femi Oyebode. 2004. Poverty, social inequity, and mental illness. *Advances in Psychiatric Treatment*, 10:216–24. http://apt.rcpsych.org/content/10/3/216.abstract (accessed January 24, 2013).

Paget, Mindie. 2003. Word power: Women's writing workshop creates soulsearching space. *Lawrence Journal-World*, April 20.

Pennebaker, James W., and Cindy K. Chang. 2011. Expressive writing: Connections to physical and mental health. In *The Oxford Handbook of Health Psychology*, ed. Howard S. Friedman, 417–36. New York: Oxford University Press.

Schneider, Pat. 2003. *Writing alone and with others*. New York: Oxford University Press.

Thunderhawk, Marilyn. Discussion with author. January 2014.

Turkheimer, Eric. 2006. Mobiles: A gloomy view of research into complex human traits. In *Wrestling with Behavioral Genetics: Science, Ethics, and Public Conversation*, eds. Erik Parens, Audrey R. Chapman, and Nancy Press, 100–108. Baltimore: Johns Hopkins University Press.

WHO (World Health Organization). 1995. *The world health report 1995: Bridging the gap*. American National Standards Institute. Geneva: WHO.

Xie, Haiyi, Gregory J. McHugo, Melinda B. Fox, and Robert E. Drake. 2005. Substance abuse relapse in a 10-year prospective follow-up with clients with mental and substance abuse disorders. *Psychiatric Services*, 56 (10):1282–87.

Yen, Hope. 2013. Single-mother families are living in poverty: Census. *Huffington Post*, September 19. http://www.huffingtonpost.com/2013/09/19/single-mother-poverty_n_3953047.html (accessed January 25, 2013).

## *Snapshot*

### Vanita Leatherwood, Baltimore, Maryland

*Writer, facilitator, and director of sexual assault and domestic violence center*

I love working with women—connecting in ways to stimulate insight, joy, and relief from sadness and stress. I also love my personal practice with creativity, even the work that isn't shared with others. The process itself creates peace for me.

I facilitate TLA workshops as part of my work as director of community engagement at HopeWorks of Howard County. HopeWorks is a sexual assault and domestic violence center. The TLA program at HopeWorks is called The Discovery Workshops. I also own Livingwell Transformative Arts, where I facilitate workshops that promote spiritual, philosophical, and social change across boundaries of age, class, culture, gender, race, and sexual orientation. Additionally, I started a creative collaborative for women called aMuseing and participate in poetry related events in the community. I also lead workshops as a volunteer for local nonprofits.

I shared my inspiration for and philosophy of my work on the Livingwell website, explaining that I choose the term "livingwell" because of how this work bolsters our personal fount of resilience: "It is the place where all our strengths are stored. It is where you will find your trust, your instincts, your smiles, your tears, your truth, your hope, your dreams and truest wishes."

www.livingwellworkshop.com

## Snapshot

### Heather Severson, Tucson, Arizona

*Writer, workshop model developer, and facilitator*

As a self-described mercenary writer and gypsy scholar, when I stumbled on the TLA Network several years ago, I found not only my tribe, but a term to describe my vocation and avocation. It's enormously satisfying to gather together with like-minded people around the challenges and rewards of practicing a livelihood in this arena.

Over many years, I've created a journal-writing practice, and from filling more than 265 notebooks processing daily life, travel, illness, dreams, and themes, I have crafted an effective method for transformational writing. The current work of my heart is shaping what I have learned into a book and a workshop curriculum, which employs kinesthetic, sensory, and other approaches to access multiple sources of creativity and self-knowledge. While it may seem counterintuitive to engage in private writing with other people, I find writing together helps people go deeper in exploring the Big Questions of our lives. Journal writing helps us develop habits of observation, reflection, meditation, movement, and playfully creating artwork in a process of inquiry, all as a way to meet our own wisdom.

www.writeitoutjournal.com

3

# Holding the Space

## *TLA Values in Education*

RUTH FARMER

Writing can seem a frivolous endeavor, a privileged action. It takes time and focus, something that too many do not have. If the goal is to get published in journals or books, the act can seem fruitless as one seeks validation in an industry that is filled with others doing the same. Yet writing can serve purposes other than reaching a large reading public.

I have journaled since I was a teenager. The sole purpose of the scribblings in those spiral-bound composition books has been to help me make sense of myself and the world in which I live. Many of my friends and acquaintances keep journals or write poems that explore confusions, joys, anger, fears, and other emotions that feel too raw to speak of, even with close friends. More than once, I have been in conversation with someone who said that writing saved her life, not because her words were read, but because they were written. I cannot say that writing saved my life, but I believe in its power. Many times the simple act of putting thoughts to paper has helped me to pay attention to my life and my world, to gain clarity and direction.

Because I value it as a path to learning in my own life, as an educator I seek to create environments in which students are encouraged to write to learn. Too often, the prime objective is for students to demonstrate their understanding of institutional or faculty worldviews or to adjust to institutional constraints—taking specific coursework in specific sequences, for example. They must produce evidence of success through receiving passing grades while in school and by acquiring appropriate jobs upon graduation. When learning is valuable in and of itself, and students can gain greater understanding about themselves and the world(s) in which they live, a larger purpose can emerge, one that moves beyond grades and jobs while taking into consideration their necessity.

There are many routes to this broader perspective on education. Applying transformative language arts (TLA) values in higher education is one way to encourage attention to learning for personal and social development. Those values are

1. personal and social transformation
2. transformation as an individual and communal process
3. defining all the defining terms
4. honoring the spoken, sung, and written word
5. interdisciplinary theory and practice
6. progressive education in theory and practice, and
7. greater perspective on your place in the world

(Goddard College, 2013, 35–36).

The TLA Network describes transformative language arts as "the intentional use of spoken, written, or sung word for social and personal transformation. This includes community building, ecological advocacy, social activism, personal growth and development, health and healing, and spiritual growth" (TLA Network, 2014). Words predominate in most educational settings, but writing is most often viewed as a mechanistic means for creating a product, usually a paper; the process is rarely attended to except in courses geared specifically to writing, such as poetry, creative writing, or composition classes. However, as Laurel Richardson notes, language is "constitutive, creating a particular view of reality and of the Self" (Richardson and St. Pierre, 2005, 960). Taking this view, the writing process must be given a more essential role in education.

In *The Courage to Teach*, Parker Palmer (1998) describes "the kind of teaching and learning space that can hold a classroom session" so that there is "creative tension." That space is bounded and open, hospitable and "charged." It allows for individual and group voices; supports solitude and provides resources; welcomes silence and speech; and honors the "big" stories of disciplines and traditions, while honoring students' "little" stories (74). Focusing on a specific Goddard College program and a capstone course in the Community College of Vermont (CCV), I demonstrate how incorporating TLA values in college settings can lead to practices that make space for creative tension, so that stories—views of reality and the Self—can emerge, and be reflected upon, opening the way for personal and social change.

Goddard College is a private school with approximately 600 students. The college's undergraduate and graduate programs are low-residency. That is, students attend intensive eight-day on-campus retreats (in Plainfield, Vermont, Port Townsend, Washington, and Seattle), followed by independent studies in collaboration with faculty advisors. CCV, a state college, serves more than 7,000 students per semester in twelve locations across Vermont and online, and it offers associates degrees and certificates. I became a CCV faculty member in 2003 and a Goddard faculty member in 2004. I currently direct the Goddard Graduate Institute, which includes three graduate programs: Health Arts & Sciences (HASMA), Social Innovation and Sustainability (MASIS), and Individualized Studies (IMA). Transformative Language Arts (TLA) is a concentration in the IMA program.

Students in the Goddard Graduate Institute and CCV are at different stages in their academic and professional journeys. At CCV, every effort is made to ensure that a student taking a class in one location receives the same quality of experience as a student taking that same class in another location, achieved through use of "essential objectives" for each course, discussed in an upcoming section. On the other hand, students who enroll in the Graduate Institute design their own courses of study. The ability to shape their own teaching and learning is a primary reason that students enroll in our programs. I will focus here on Goddard's IMA program generally and, specifically, the Transformative Language Arts concentration within IMA, and on CCV's Seminar in Educational Inquiry to show that, despite their different educational approaches, the values incorporated in TLA can create and hold spaces so that students may travel their own paths toward academic and personal growth.

# Personal and Social Transformation: Individual and Communal Processes

A leader is one who holds the space for the brilliance of others.

*—Marianne Williamson (2012, 108)*

As a program director, I am in contact with students from their initial inquiries through graduation and, often, beyond. Phone calls, e-mails, applications, interviews, new student orientations, monitoring student progress, and interacting with alumni have given me a broad perspective of the range of learners that are attracted to Goddard. Frequently, students' professional and academic goals resonate with Goddard's mission "to advance cultures of rigorous inquiry, collaboration and lifelong learning, where individuals take imaginative and responsible action in the world" (Goddard College, 2012). The college's mission is in concert with IMA's mission, which states, in part:

> Graduate studies in the program are aimed at the integration of knowledge, personal development, and social action. . . . The mission of the MA in Individualized Studies program is to foster the development of knowledge, practices, and modes of inquiry that represent a genuine attempt to offer new perspectives, in a world affected by huge transformative forces. (Goddard College, 2013, 6)

TLA concentrators (TLAers) delve into knowledge, practices, and modes of inquiry through singing, writing, or performance. Social action is an important aspect of TLA practice:

> To truly see TLA as a force that can transform communities, you are encouraged to look toward local and global social movements, how social change happens, and what you define as social change. By exploring TLA as a tool for political, economic, and social change, you also develop more approaches for helping individuals and communities free themselves from the roots of what silences them, and seek greater means of sharing and celebrating their stories. (Goddard College, 2013, 41)

You might say that TLAers expect to demonstrate "Big C" Change, in the way that Howard Gardner refers to Big C Creativity (Gardner, 1999, 117); that is, change that impacts a domain or area (which could be a community, a family, a country), shifts people's worldviews, and challenges and, ultimately, changes dominant paradigms.

Even before they enroll in our program, TLAers frequently have developed a practice. They come to us as teachers, singers, poets, writers, workshop facilitators, and community organizers who use words or writing processes for their own growth and to encourage growth in others. They enroll in TLA to build a stronger theoretical foundation for their practices. They seek mentors to challenge them and help them to deepen their knowledge of their fields of inquiry. They come to acquire new skills and to explore issues in dialogue with others. Other Graduate Institute students hale from similar backgrounds: professionals who seek an intellectual community in which they can develop professionally.

From their first residency, Graduate Institute students encounter the "bounded and open" spaces of

- new student orientation activities that urge them to explore their rationale for pursuing a graduate degree, while becoming familiar with degree requirements;
- advising groups, during which their faculty advisors and peers—through "hospitable and 'charged'" dialogue—assist them in developing semester study plans;
- workgroups that encourage expansive thinking while plotting a path toward a thesis-driven final product that meets degree requirements.

The faculty advisor is the most intimate teacher because students work one-on-one with them, but student learning also takes place through skills- or content-based workshops led by staff, faculty, students, and visiting scholars, as well as through informal conversations over meals and in the dorms. These experiences create multiple opportunities to dialogue about issues that are meaningful to our community.

Faculty and I seek to motivate and empower students so that they understand that their goals and objectives have substance and value. They are the subjects of their stories. They are also the authors of their stories, and these stories are large because they have such deep impact in the students' lives. Some recent areas of studies in the Graduate Institute have included the following: gender studies, death and dying, nonprofit management, urban ecology, positive psychology, Eastern philosophy, queer studies, medical anthropology, solidarity economies, community health, and systems thinking.

Through the process of developing semester study plans—which requires research, reflection, articulating study rationales and goals, writing, and revising—students gain confidence in speaking and writing about the things that are most meaningful in their lives. Through intellectual exchanges with advisors and peers, they learn how to articulate their positions and to engage multiple and opposing viewpoints. Thus their individual learning takes place in collaboration with a supportive learning community. All students are required to undertake a practicum, internships, fieldwork, or other engaged practice so that they may apply their theories in the real world. Because they will complete the bulk of their research and studies in their communities, what they learn may have deeper meaning than meeting degree criteria. Although Goddard does get students who "just want a degree," most want a degree and something more.

Documentation of their learning (called "packets") may include audiovisual texts, such as photographs or music; however, the predominant medium is writing. Through their written feedback, faculty encourage students toward more sophisticated explorations and articulations, and they urge them to consider historical and cultural contexts, particularly those that are different from their own. Faculty packet response letters provide resources, questions, provocations, mentorship, and direction. In the spirit of Marianne Williamson, faculty "hold the space for the brilliance" of our students (2012, 108).

Though the program is individualized, it has structure and degree criteria.[1] The ways in which students meet the criteria are determined by students' intentions, goals, and objectives, rather than the institution's or faculty's. As such, earning a degree may lead to professional advancement or jobs, but the program also serves as a vehicle for creating/building upon a chosen Life. Faculty and I support students as they develop projects that impact lives; the impact comes from moving beyond the theoretical to transforming words into action.

## Defining All the Defining Terms[2]

Reconfigure your dominant scholarly paradigms and, presto, you reconfigure the very phenomena you are examining. This is also the first commandment of postmodernism: We see what we believe; we observe what we narrate; we transform what we reframe.

—*Nash (2004, 45)*

Students often come to Goddard prepared to study and convey their own worldviews. They are willing, and perhaps eager, to believe that "we transform what we reframe." This perspective is perhaps a bit solipsistic. We might transform the ways in which we view a thing—idea, theory, belief. However, the thing itself isn't transformed magically just because we think about it differently or reframe our beliefs using academic language. Ideas, theories, beliefs, paradigms, and more are reframed through action, moving from knowing to doing. In the process of that doing, the student may shift his or her perspectives. Two examples:

- A student started the program exploring the connections between place and identity; her final product posited that consciousness is created with place.
- A student started by wanting to study ghost stories; the final product explored the socially invisible, victims of sex trafficking.

Through research, talking with peers, and engaging communities, the students transformed their understanding of their fields of inquiry. Their own changes may not have been the primary point but rather a collateral consequence of their collaborative learning. Faculty do not determine whether students have "transformed." Students articulate their personal and/or professional transformations in multiple ways, such as reflective essays, critical analyses, engaged practices, and final products.

# Honoring the Spoken, Sung, and Written Word

In 2003, the National Commission on Writing in America's Schools and Colleges published "The Neglected 'R': The Need for a Writing Revolution," a report on the state of writing in the United States. The report's basic premise was that "American education will never realize its potential as an engine of opportunity and economic growth until a writing revolution puts language and communication in their proper place in the classroom" (National Commission on Writing, 2003, 3). Writing was recognized as "a richly elaborated logically connected amalgam of ideas, words, themes, images, and multimedia designs" (13), and the commission put forth five recommendations: (1) place writing at the center of school agenda; (2) increase the amount of time students spend writing; (3) create authentic assessments of writing; (4) use appropriate emerging technologies in teaching and learning writing; and (5) provide professional development so that all teachers may learn how to incorporate writing into their courses (26–32).

In the Graduate Institute, writing is a primary means of communication among students and faculty, so students are required to spend a great deal of time writing. Faculty committees assess student writing through review of progress portfolios and thesis proposals. The use of technologies varies among faculty, as does professional development. Still, we are an example of an institution that views language and communication as essential to learning. Writing goes beyond producing packets to document learning. Process letters and reflective essays are means of inquiry. Though the final products of TLAers are most likely to center around language, other students in the Graduate Institute have brought words into the center of their areas of study. For example, a student's final product was a CD focusing on archetypes; another produced a theatre piece about father absence. TLAers have written memoirs, poetry collections, and scholarly essays.

Explicitly or implicitly, students and faculty understand, as Richardson notes, that "language is how social organization and power are defined and contested and the place where one's sense of self—one's subjectivity—is constructed. Understanding language as competing discourses—competing ways of giving meaning and of organizing the world—makes language a site of exploration and struggle" (Richardson and St. Pierre, 2005, 961).

## Interdisciplinary Theory and Progressive Education in Practice: Taking It Online

Online classes and fully online degrees have proliferated in the past few years. Given the ready availability of the Internet, such delivery models have been for many the difference between obtaining a degree and not. Though it offers convenience, online learning can be difficult. According to Palloff and Pratt (2003), the ideal online student should have access to a computer and the Internet and the skills to use them, is open-minded about sharing details about their lives, is comfortable expressing themselves in an environment that lacks visual and audio cues, is self-motivated and disciplined, can work collaboratively to build a learning community, and is a critical thinker and writer (5–8). Needless to say, as in any learning situation, there are students who do not fall into the "ideal" category. Sometimes the simplest of techniques can help a student become more engaged and, ultimately, more successful in this environment. One technique I used was to change the setting on the discussion forum of my online CCV course, Seminar in Educational Inquiry (SEI).

SEI is a capstone course that I have taught for ten years, face-to-face, hybrid, and now fully online. As with all CCV courses, the curriculum is guided by essential objectives (EOs)[3] intended to help students meet the Vermont State College graduation standards in writing and information literacy. The culminating project is a research paper that must earn a grade of C- or better in order for the student to pass the course. In my course, the final research paper is more than a means for producing a quantifiable product. Students choose their own research topics and are urged to choose a topic that sparks their curiosity.

Through scaffolded assignments, they develop the paper over several weeks and are offered multiple opportunities to apply and strengthen research and writing skills while investigating topics they are passionate about. They explore a range of disciplines throughout the semester, including those in the natural sciences, social sciences, and the humanities, by reading essays, journal articles, newspaper items, and book chapters and by viewing short videos or documentaries. Topics include the nature of creativity, identity development, ethics and values, ways of knowing, and the environment. They write papers and reflect on texts predominantly through the discussion forums. The forums have the added benefit of giving them practice in critical reading, writing, and reflection, thus further preparing them to successfully complete their final papers.

Like Graduate Institute students, writing is a central means of learning. However, instead of self-designed courses of study, course descriptions and EOs frame CCV students' education. Syllabi and weekly schedules guide their learning through the semester. The teaching methods, documentation of learning, and the weight of each assignment are outlined for them. Unlike the low-residency model, faculty and students do not meet face-to-face, and the printed word with the occasional emoticon are the only cues to a writer's affect. Given the relative anonymity of the environment, creating a safe intellectual space is essential.

On discussion forums, the most prolific or articulate student frequently dominates the conversation, unless the instructor assertively opens the space for less skillful or more reticent students. CCV's learning management system is Moodle, an open-source platform that offers several forum settings; the most commonly used one is Standard, which allows anyone in the class to post a question at any time. During my first year teaching online, I used the Standard setting. Typically, the week's discussions were initiated by someone with lots to say about the topic or the reading. Class members would invariably respond to that person's opinions/reflections, rather than offering their own. Dialogues more easily devolved into engaging with one or two posts, thus limiting the exploration of multiple views. It was difficult to know what individual students thought because too many abandoned their ideas, choosing to reflect back what others said. To counter single-view dialogues or arguments, I would insert questions and provocations. (It is amazing how frequently I was ignored. There is a research project in this: Do students consider an instructor a member of the class?) My belief is that too many students lack the confidence, initiative, and skill to shift dialogues. Rather, it is easier to say as little as possible or say nothing at all if the conversation isn't conducive to broader perspectives. It can be rather nerve-wracking to step into the void and express an opinion before knowing where others stand, especially if you disagree. Doing so on a discussion forum can render the act permanent, more of a declaration than the opening gambit to a conversation or a responsible reflection on an opposing view.

In her book *Quiet: The Power of Introverts in a World That Can't Stop Talking*, Susan Cain cites studies on the impact of group collaboration. In one 2005 study, neuroscientist Gregory Berns asked volunteers to play a decision-making game. As they played, their brains were scanned. Berns discovered that individuals gave wrong answers an average of 13.8 percent of the time when working alone. When they played with a group in which wrong answers were given, they agreed with the group 41 percent of the time. Most significant was that the scan showed that conformists had less activity in the frontal, decision-making areas of the brain. They were not consciously abandoning their beliefs to fit in. Rather, there was more activity in the areas that control perception. That is, the group actually changed individuals' views on the problems, even though the group perception was incorrect (2012, 91–92). My online students' consistent (and repetitive) agreement with a few class members' perspectives bore this out.

At the opposite end of the spectrum were those students who saw every statement as an opportunity for dispute and taking the moral high ground. A student once told me that she felt it was her responsibility to show that hers was the right perspective. She was also one of the students who felt put out when I switched to the Q&A setting—she wanted to know what others had to say *before* she posted. I guess forewarned is forearmed when an interaction is viewed as a battle of wits.

The Q&A setting requires students to respond to the instructor's initial post before they are allowed to read other class members' responses. This setting allows students to express their own ideas before wading into the fray and allows me to hold a space for students to engage their own thinking independent of group-think. In face-to-face classes, teachers can encourage students with follow-up questions and comments that support differential ways of knowing, conversation styles, or perspectives. Body language and facial expressions alert class members that someone wants to speak. Students can interject questions and comments to immediate effect. The dialogue takes on many shapes: spider web, spiral, circle, triangles, or quadrangles in a flow of words connecting speaker to speaker. Or the dialogue can become like the cartoon with an empty bubble above everyone's head, as we struggle to come up with the next thing. Such empty space is not possible online and the dialogue is visually, if not actually, linear.

A simple technique like changing the discussion forum setting has led to more detailed, innovative, and thought-provoking responses. It has created a more collaborative environment and allowed students to take charge of their education by stepping out and naming their own experiences as they relate to the topics at hand. Students are more engaged with each other, and a range of ideas emerges from the onset of the discussion. Some of the less-than-committed students reply by apologizing for being late or offering other chitchat; then they can see their peers' responses. That is rare, however.

I explore this very simple tool at such length because it made room for more people to enter the conversation in more complex ways. When using the Standard setting, the typical initial responses began with "I agree" or "I like the way you . . ." Now students' initial responses explore the discussion questions or readings. They place what they have learned in context with their own thinking. I did not change my questions; I merely altered the method through which students entered the dialogue. By compelling them to engage directly with the text first, students' responses shifted to deeper analysis and synthesis. They quote texts, compare and contrast theories/experiences found in different readings, or explore their ideas in terms of the authors'. They are also more inclined to extend the dialogue by asking questions and by providing additional resources, such as YouTube videos or links to newspaper articles. In keeping with progressive education, students take charge of their own learning and are more collaborative.

## Greater Perspective on Your Place in the World

Making space for students to express themselves seems self-evident until you are faced with groups of students who are reluctant to participate because they doubt their intellect. I was gratified to receive an e-mail from a student who was initially dismayed at not having access to classmates' posts before posting her reading responses. She thanked me for the class, and said that the Q&A setting helped her to gain confidence in her own thinking. That is what I had intended. This same student focused her final paper on the importance of sunscreen. As a health worker in a dermatologist's office and a fair-skinned person, she understood firsthand the problems that emerge from overexposure to sun.

Many students write papers that emerge from personal or professional experiences: Some recent papers have dealt with outsourcing, water pollution, alternative healing modalities, juvenile incarceration, and childhood vaccinations. In the larger scheme of things, this course might seem to have nothing to do with social change or transformation. However, it is through these small, seemingly routine experiences that we learn who we are and how we function in society. Writing a research paper is not a lofty goal unless it is the first time you've been asked to write about something that is meaningful in your life. Just being able to choose can be transformative. For some students, finding and exploring their interests can be daunting, so I generally support students' choice of topic. I am most interested in helping them develop the skills to articulate their primary stance on the topic and support that position with solid research, multiple/opposing views, and coherent writing. Handouts, mini-lectures, and links to resources, as well as written feedback and evaluation at each stage, support students' independent work.

At this educational level, transformation might be as simple as understanding that the instructor really does want to know what students think, or understanding that it is okay to disagree with the sources that they include in their papers. These might not be life-saving changes; however, learning to express oneself in writing, to articulate ideas such that others may understand thought processes, these are important personal and academic markers. Once words are written/spoken, readers/listeners can reflect upon them, embrace them, reject them, reshape them, ignore them, misquote them. Holding the space for these explorations requires maintaining safe intellectual environments. It is an important job for an educator.

Depending on with whom you speak when you ask about the purpose of higher education, you will receive different answers. I believe that higher education is a means through which people develop as thinkers and learners and become informed global citizens. In a recent blog post, Duke University professor Cathy Davidson wrote that she wanted to frame an upcoming talk around the question: "What if we thought of higher education as preparation to be a world changer, in any sphere you choose, in whatever profession you aspire to?" She goes on to write:

> What if we thought of higher education as the way to help prepare you for the best, most productive, most satisfying, most constructive contribution you could make to helping the world be a better place? *What if we set the bar that high?*
>
> What would change about higher education if that were the goal?
>
> What if we said the cost of a college education is so worth it because, when you graduate, you have the tool kit for changing your world in some meaningful way? (Davidson, 2014)

Applying the values that guide transformative language arts practices can shift this scenario from "what if" to reality. The intentional focus upon language, interdisciplinary theory and practice, and progressive pedagogy help students to develop as thinkers, writers, and change agents. Words might not save lives, but they certainly encourage us toward a broader understanding of and collaboration with various communities, which are the first steps toward meaningful social change.

1. To meet degree criteria, students must
    1. identify and master disciplines central to their specific study;
    2. place their learning in an appropriate historical, cultural, and personal context;
    3. explore and reflect upon their values, biases, and social, cultural, spiritual and ideological roots as these pertain to their area of study;
    4. engage with the world through a personal, social, spiritual, or other practice appropriate to the individual study; and
    5. complete a final product that demonstrates their mastery of the traditions and disciplines pertinent to their study, and demonstrates their learning, personal growth, and engaged practice.

    (Goddard College, 2013, 6–7)

2. "Defining all the defining terms as part of TLA's philosophy comes from the understanding that true transformation only comes when the ones transformed can claim and name their own experience" (Goddard College, 2013, 35).

3. By the end of SEI, students must be able to

    1. Explain how questions are framed and knowledge is gained through various methods of inquiry including: the scientific method, statistical analysis of data, research, literature, and the process of writing and dialogue.
    2. Investigate the philosophical and ethical questions arising from issues pertaining to identity, community, knowledge, truth, change and responsibility.
    3. Focus written work around an explicit or an implied central thesis a position statement or proposition advanced by the writer that is arguable and supportable and develop the thesis systematically, using specific details and relevant supporting evidence.
    4. Demonstrate advanced skills of reading, writing and critical thinking in both group and individual work.
    5. Collect, organize, critically evaluate and properly cite information, utilizing a variety of traditional and electronic resources.
    6. Design, compose and revise a final paper that includes an implied or explicit thesis statement, integrates relevant source material from five or more credible sources, and demonstrates proficiency in the graduation standards of writing and information literacy by achieving a grade of C- or better.

    (Farmer, 2014)

## References


Cain, Susan. 2012. *Quiet: The power of the introvert in a world that won't stop talking*. New York: Crown.

Davidson, Cathy. 2014. What if the goal of higher education was to make world changers. Blog. https://www.hastac.org/blogs/cathy-davidson/2014/03/11/what-if-goal-higher-education-was-make-world-changers (accessed March 2014).

Farmer, Ruth. 2014. Spring syllabus. Seminar in Educational Inquiry.

Gardner, Howard. 1999. *Intelligence reframed: Multiple intelligences for the 21st century*. New York: Basic Books.

Goddard College. Fall 2013. Individualized MA Studies Program Graduate Student Addendum Handbook.

——. 2012. Mission Statement. http://goddard.edu/about-goddard/goddard-difference (accessed March 3, 2014).

Nash, Robert. 2004. *Liberating scholarly writing: The power of personal narratives.* New York: Teachers College Press.

National Commission on Writing in America's Schools and Colleges. 2003. The neglected "R": The need for a writing revolution. *The College Board.* http://www.californiawritingproject.org/uploads/1/3/6/0/13607033/neglectedr.pdf (accessed April 9, 2014).

Palloff, Rena, and Keith Pratt. 2003. *The virtual student: Profiles and guide to working with online learners.* San Francisco: John Wiley.

Palmer, Parker J. 1998. *The courage to teach: Exploring the inner landscape of a teacher's life.* San Francisco: Jossey-Bass.

Richardson, Laurel, and Elizabeth Adams St. Pierre. 2005. Writing: A method of inquiry. In *The Sage Handbook of Qualitative Research,* 3rd ed., 959–78. Thousand Oaks, CA: Sage.

TLA Network. 2014. http://www.tlanetwork.org/about/what-is-tlan/.

Williamson, Marianne. 2012. *The law of divine compensation: On work, money, and miracles.* New York: HarperCollins.

# Snapshot

**Patricia Fontaine, Shelburne, Vermont**

*Writer and facilitator of workshops for people living with cancer*

In 2007, I began to offer Healing Writing workshops for cancer patients that had the added value of offering simple artistic expression to broaden and deepen the insights and revelations that arrived during the writing part of class. I currently teach a free weekly drop-in class for folks dealing with illness and their caregivers, called Healing Art & Writing, that uses simple tools of expressive writing and art to arrive at fresh insights on the nature of healing and living well with illness. I also offer writing workshops for women in transition, people living with cancer, and those navigating as physically different in the world.

Every single week after class I reflect on what a privilege it is to witness extraordinarily ordinary people discover and engage their creativity with depth, huge heart, and enormous courage. I often joke with them that "everything I need to know in life I learned from my students." In their presence I have learned all over again "that art is worthless / unless it plants / a measure of splendor in people's hearts" (from "Twigs," by Taja Muhammad Ali).

Inspired by my students every day, I worked with them to publish a collection of their art and writing with a stealth mission: being on every coffee table in every treatment setting in the county to inspire new patients that they too can use their illness as rich ground for creativity. The book, which we published *for* members of our class and others in the *community*, is titled *Healing Art & Writing: Using Creativity to Meet Illness, A Collection of Student Work from 2009 to 2011*. It has had positive responses from waiting patients and was thrilling for students to engage with.

www.patriciafontaine.com/

# *Snapshot*

## **Nancy Morgan, Washington, DC**

*Arts and Humanities director at Georgetown Lombardi Comprehensive Cancer Center*

I have applied the lessons of my TLA master's work directly and unedited to a hospital community, engaging people with cancer and their caregivers as well as medical and support staff throughout the hospital in expressive writing to find balance, direction, meaning, and physical and emotional relief.

For thirteen years, as the Arts and Humanities director at the Georgetown Lombardi Comprehensive Cancer Center, I have sought ways to teach, advocate, facilitate, and scientifically validate the health benefits of writing. The greatest challenge is helping people see writing as play rather than work and overcoming the resistance to write, fear of ridicule, of not measuring up. Expressive writing exposes vulnerabilities. We backpedal through all the apologies and excuses until the words are out there, in the air, acknowledged, embraced.

I love surprising clients—illiterate folks to published writers—with the joy and cathartic effect of expressive writing. Expressing thoughts and feelings is not culturally supported. People must be invited to bare their soul, and the result is immense gratitude and the courage to write again.

www.lombardi.georgetown.edu/artsandhumanities

4

# *Youth, Writing, and Identity*

## *An Interview with Sarah W. Bartlett*

RUTH FARMER

*Poet and writer Sarah W. Bartlett, MPH, ScD, is owner/director of Women Writing for (a) Change—Vermont, LLC. She is also co-founder of writinginsideVT, a weekly writing program at the Chittenden Regional Correctional Facility in South Burlington, Vermont. I interviewed Sarah in her homey, four-room studio in Burlington. The place is filled with pillows, colorful cloths, paintings, books, and posters created by the women affiliated with Women Writing for (a) Change.*

RUTH: Tell us something about your life as a professional writer.

SARAH: Like the lupine lady, I want to leave the world a more beautiful place. So having beauty emerge from and pass through my hands gives me great satisfaction, connects others with the handmade life, and helps slow down the frantic pace of life about and within me. I am passionate about living in harmony with Earth and helping the marginalized among us find voice. This passion can take the form of intensity—doing too much for others, doing too much, period. It can also take the form of dogged determination—to make a point, get something done against all odds, forge ahead when reason, logic, and good sense would suggest stopping. It can mean being a stickler for process because I have witnessed, over and over, the tremendous power of silence, deep listening, equal voice in a circle. It can at times feel overbearing to those less passionate, dedicated, or experienced; it can also intrigue and invite participation and discovery. Above all, my passion keeps me present, engaged, and moving forward. The values and tools that compose Women Writing for (a) Change allow me to share my passion in a way that supports and draws out a kindred passion in others.

My true aim in my work is to midwife women in their process of crafting a more conscious way of living through the art of writing and practices of community. The path I have chosen to achieve it is through writing with and facilitating a community of women called Women Writing for (a) Change—Vermont. This work continues to issue outward into additional settings. I am most called to women reentering from incarceration and healing from illness; girls, teens, and young women seeking their voice; and ways of doing this work that bring together different groups and multiple expressive modalities.

RUTH: You have worked with Women Writing for (a) Change for a number of years and direct your own site. Tell us about this organization and what drew you to it.

SARAH: Established in 1991 in Cincinnati, Ohio, by Mary Pierce Brosmer, Women Writing for (a) Change offers carefully structured containers to encourage becoming-conscious women to come to voice. In the early 1990s, this was a novelty for many of us closet writers. I vividly recall my initiation to the group at a November reading in 1993. I did not realize there were women like me for whom writing was a form of breathing. Even more, I had no idea that it was possible to come together and learn from one another.

RUTH: What happened during that first encounter that shifted you from a closet writer to someone who publishes and who mentors other writers?

SARAH: It was like coming home. I heard from women who used writing to express, learn, teach one another, understand themselves. It was a totally novel experience—it was like hearing myself in the stories of others. I didn't know it was about finding a voice—I didn't have that language at the time. But my response poured itself into a poem I shared once joining the Wednesday-night group in January 1994. Ever since, I have been a regular writer and active participant in all aspects of the Cincinnati school. I was part of the brainstorming for the young women's program in the later 1990s and a regular summer retreatant. I took an early leadership role within the weekly circle and became the anthologist for classes and retreats. As Women Writing for (a) Change went through significant growth in those early years, I was honored to be part of the original core of writers.

After I moved to Vermont in 1997, I stayed in close touch with Mary Pierce Brosmer and the Wednesday-night writers. During the summer of 2003, more than ten years into the school, Mary laid plans for her sabbatical year: to create a training for women to carry the *charism* of Women Writing out to other cities across the country. The timing worked well for me: my firstborn went to college that fall, leaving me feeling somewhat at loose ends. So when the program started in January 2004, I signed up as Mary's assistant. This first group of trainees became known as the "pioneers" of the fledgling Feminist Leadership Academy, which has since, and more accurately, become known as the Conscious Feminine Leadership Academy. That is indeed the underlying thread of Women Writing for (a) Change: *to become more conscious in our leadership and lives through the art of writing and practices of community.*

RUTH: Tell us about the Women Writing for (a) Change process. How does it differ from other writing workshops or writing circles?

SARAH: Two things stand out in answer to this question. First is that although we "workshop" one another's writing (and yes, I am an equal in the circle as both writer and feedback giver), we do *not* offer "critique." We take time at the start of each semester to learn different ways to request focused feedback and to give the feedback that is requested. Mary very wisely wanted to avoid her own early experiences of being put down by "experts." Women Writing for (a) Change works on the principle of listening with respect and openness. We help the writer dream her dream onward rather than imposing our own ideas of what the writing should be. Ultimately the writing belongs to the writer.

The second major difference from other writing groups is that we embody underlying conscious feminine principles in our practices as well as our intention. We intentionally create a community that practices going slowly, thinking before we speak, reflecting, taking responsibility for our words and our behavior, treating each other as equals and with mutual respect, avoiding competition or negative comparisons. Our intent is to lift up what is strong and true in each other's writing. We create and hold space for truth-telling that need not be distorted to match another's expectations.

RUTH: You have facilitated classes, workshops, and retreats for adult women writers and for young women writers. How did your work with one group inform your work with the other?

SARAH: For the first three years, I worked only with adult women as a purely pragmatic matter. In order to introduce the Vermont community to Women Writing, it seemed important to create a core group of women invested in our practices and community. Second, that provided an entrée to young women. I figured once mothers had experienced the magic, they'd be eager to have their daughters in on it as well. And finally, it required invested adults to fund the younger generation. As an independent provider, I rely solely on fees to support the program. For ten years the program has been entirely self-sustaining; for about 80 percent of that time, we've been able to support dedicated studio space. I am very proud of the fact of self-sufficiency, especially in the face of all it has given the community.

So there were the practical aspects of locating interested women and girls, and guaranteeing that the fees would be paid. Beyond that, I was able to tap into the mothers' wistfulness to have had such a safe space of their own to explore the unique issues of girls growing up. As the mother of two teenage daughters myself, I was familiar with many of these, of course. Thus, mothers became silent partners in the design of the Saturday workshops and summer camps. I was able to weave in things they wished they had been able to explore in a safe, constructive, and caring community when younger, adding in the perspectives of current mothers along with the many challenges facing girls growing up today.

It would also be fair to say that some of the perspectives offered by the young women who came to our circles prompted me to explore memories and childhood situations among my adult writers that may have gotten lost over the years. So much in these young women is fresh and hopeful and free-flowing. It saddens me that we spend so much of our adult years trying to recapture the creative freedom of our youth. So yes, the girls inspired me to select some of the themes for my adult groups: writing from the body, for instance. Or the importance of place. I always loved when a ten- or thirteen-year-old girl started her writing with "when I was little . . ."

RUTH: What were some of the suggestions you received from adult women?

SARAH: Sometimes mothers shared privately their concerns for a daughter who suffered from poor self-esteem, who longed to be creative but felt limited by school curricula, who was clearly talented and needed an outlet, who suffered from social anxiety and needed a positive group experience.

Topics of concern to girls at that age are body image, having a voice, what it means to be a woman, how you develop self-confidence and self-esteem, bullying, how creativity can save you, permission to be unique, standing up for personal beliefs, the environment. These themes would weave through their writing in response to specific prompts. Peer pressures to have sex, drink, or do drugs were not explicit topics, but prompts often allowed girls to explore and discuss these things if they were on their minds.

There were also girls who just wanted to become better writers. When parents spoke after group read-arounds, we heard over and over how proud they were of the self-confidence and courage of their daughters. For some, this was a transformative experience—many just wanted to stay in the writing circle and not leave! In a group of girls they did not go to school with, they found immediate commonalities and were able to produce some remarkably deep writing.

RUTH: Describe the retreats with young women writers. For example, who attended? What were their goals? What were your goals?

SARAH: I held five consecutive summer camps for about a dozen middle-school-age girls. They came from a wide number of area schools. This was an intentional decision, as I wanted to avoid the kinds of conflict that can arise when girls from the same school bring their cliquishness to summer groups. Snubbing/judgment is strictly forbidden within our groups, but when it arrives full-blown there is no room in a five-day program to defuse it entirely. Furthermore, I wanted to create a community of young women that transcended geographical boundaries. In each group, I tried to have girls from less advantaged homes writing and creating alongside those with intact families and privilege.

I think it fair to say each girl came with some expectation that her writing would improve, that she would learn skills, such as how to write a particular kind of poem or to revise a work she either brought from home or started Monday. In addition, they each knew that creating a strong community was a key part of our work. We had clear agreements about how we would interact—no judgment about one another's words or lives, no putting self down, equality in the circle, including we facilitators who always wrote and shared with the girls. And, of course, they came to have fun.

Our goals were to help teens enhance self-esteem, build skills in creative self-expression, learn to receive and give honest support and encouragement, develop skills in building and maintaining community, and seek and recognize role models who inspire creative life choices. In our camps and classes, we created a supportive community of writers, wrote together and on our own, shared our writing and listened to one another, explored other modes of artistic expression, read and discussed stories, articles, and poems. Camp themes over the years have included:

- Strong women/fairy tales/media messages/revolutionary self
- Creation stories/ecology/Earth Day/women and nature
- Metaphor/dream/mandala/character development
- Sisterhood/girls speak out/leadership/problem-solving/peace
- Naming/stereotypes/body image/intuition/our true nature

Overall, I'd say their goals were to have fun with writing and to learn writing skills. They also learned how to work with new people, how to ask for and give helpful/respectful feedback, and how to inhabit their voices. Each week ended with some kind of group project. One year we made nature mandalas from found objects by the lake; this was the year we focused on Mother Nature/our own nature. Another year they created a door-size collage of photos they had taken, words they had spoken during the week, and a poem they created from their own lines. They wanted to show strong, activist women in the making. And always, we created an anthology of work from the week—the first few in print, the final few on CDs. This way they could have all the writings AND all the photos.

Young Women Writing for (a) Change means the chance for community, challenge, and growth: deepening into writing, deepening into self. The girls who shared this circle are amazing young women—adventuresses, heartfelt seekers, caring sisters, insightful, humorous, sensitive, and—above all—*talented.* This poem was created from the April 2009 Saturday group's writing:

**Young Women Writing for (a) Change—Vermont**

The circle forms an environment of relaxation and love
after we start writing, sharing, talking,
a community of different people, bonded by love to write—and a candle.
In this sacred home of words and laughter,
escaping into one another's story worlds,
a door has opened.
I feel strong, secure and ready
calm, relaxed and hopeful
creative juices flowing from my heart through pen then spilling onto
paper
a world of magic and mystery
depth and courage
knowing it will be kept safe
not be judged.

So much hope, beautiful honesty
these amazing young women
brave enough to step up to new levels,
a new voice deepening into writing, into self.
School does not provide this.

Come to learn about yourself and your state of mind;
We are peace, calm, smart, pure, natural young women
grown and blossomed, confident, shiny and contented.
Confidence has grown within and around each girl
I cannot help but smile—time flies, we are all having fun.
Thank you for this uplifting experience
this chance for community, challenge and growth.

At camp, we always read together just after lunch—kind of like rest time, a break from creating, interacting; just a chance to take in. Sometimes we read short stories or articles, each complementing the day's specific component of the larger theme for the week.

In the last couple of summers, we decided to read an entire book. So the week we worked with nature—Gaia stories, the Earth and its stewardship, our own internal natures and personal challenges—we read *Island of the Blue Dolphin*, by Scott O'Dell. The week we focused on community—voice and silence, leadership and change—we read excerpts from *The Secret Life of Bees*, by Sue Monk Kidd, in order to get through it in just a few readings. As with our opening poems and exercises, lines from the book were used as writing prompts. We structured the week so each day focused on a quality. For instance, Wednesday it was contemplation and reflection, so we took a field trip to a nearby outdoor labyrinth. We spent the afternoon there writing in silence. It gave them several layers of experience, including one not unlike May's wall in the book. The labyrinth became the metaphor for the week: what we brought of our selves, what expectations going in, and what we took back out when we left.

Life is a labyrinth.
Long and winding.
Twists and turns mark the
Changing path of
Humanity.
KF 7/12

We also read selections from a number of other books, including *Meeting at the Crossroads*, *The Art of Dreaming*, by Jill Mellick, *Gather the Women, Save the World: Urgent Message from Mother*, by Jean Shinoda Bolen, as well as using lines from them as additional writing prompts.

RUTH: Working with teens can be exhilarating and difficult. What kinds of activities occurred during the writing retreats that helped these girls develop the focus to write, and give feedback?

SARAH: We would start each day with games and ice breakers. For example, on the first day we would toss a ball across the circle, and the recipient had to name herself. Then we switched it around, naming the girl first and tossing the ball to her, going faster and faster. This is a lively way to learn names quickly. We started with a different game each morning, to get the juices flowing. Sometimes it was an improv game that moved around the circle.

Writing took place in small and discrete chunks of time and space. Fast-writing to prompts after the initial game, then writing in pairs or small groups to create a play or song or interactive story using characters each had developed alone, for instance. Or writing after reading, reflecting on the story by starting with a line from it, or in response to a question posed, or linking it to personal experience. Later in the afternoon, we generally worked on a group art project. Each week ended with an anthology of writing, so gathering pieces and typing them up was another activity. And the last day, we invited parents, family, and friends to a modest reading to let them know what we had been working on.

Physical activity took place every day, between games, swimming, and movement from space to space. We could write outside, throw Frisbees, do yoga, or dance. We provided both stimulation and quiet, constantly aware of changing pace as needed. One summer was brutally hot. We held camp at a private home without air conditioning. But there was a pool. We had a lot of watermelon and water breaks that summer, but they hung in there. My favorite photo from that year was of one girl who insisted she keep on writing even while trying to cool off—in the pool.

In addition to writing multiple times per day, both to prompts and to/with one another in small groups, each program had both its own theme and some kind of expressive art form. For instance, the first camp (which was held at the Women's Center at St. Michael's College) featured a daily swim at the college pool and afternoon stone carving. The stonework became a powerful metaphor, which the girls used in a variety of other ways, too—such as composing their own collective song from the week's words. In our final two summers, we had our own dedicated writing studio just ten minutes from Oakledge Park in Burlington. So we spent a couple of hours at midday swimming and picnicking, during which we read a book that was part of the week-long theme.

RUTH: Did the girls gravitate to particular genres?

SARAH: They seemed most drawn to poetry and fiction.

RUTH: When you think of the phrase "transformative language arts," what comes to mind, and how does this resonate with what you do in your work with Women Writing for (a) Change?

SARAH: By definition, creative writing is, I believe, transformative. The very act of writing leads you to discover what lies within. In my experience as a creative writer, you do not sit down to record something already conceived. Rather, the process of writing itself unveils or shapes what is inside waiting to be released, discovered. And writing offers the chance to go back over time and reread, compare, learn from what was written before. In that comparison, you can see change (or not), can glean how circumstance has impacted you, how you approach similar situations. You can learn about yourself and, with the tool of writing in hand, can write your way to healing, growth, change.

RUTH: I wonder if people would agree that "by definition, writing is transformative." I'm fairly certain that people *do* sit down to create something already conceived. I consider formulaic types of writing, such as crime novels, or romances, or self-help books. Perhaps I'm misunderstanding the term "already conceived."

SARAH: I should say the writing that we do—personal creative writing, much of it in the moment. I never talk about formulaic writing, unless you consider writing formal poetry that follows syllables and rhyme schemes to be formulaic. I'm talking about writing that is a free exploration. You are given a prompt and write for ten minutes. You learn something, some understanding becomes clear. You work it further and it becomes something else. Maybe you would call it open-ended writing. About twenty minutes in, something usually starts to happen. After that, some gem sort of sparkles, some inner wisdom or learning, or something that is transformative. And often, the end is far from where it started. The following poem was created by the girls from their writing during the week together. To me, it speaks directly to the kinds of social change they are in the process of embodying:

> Let's begin again,
> a reason to weave ordinary words together.
> We must be motivated to instigate ambition.

When I used to dream, I dreamt of terror
hidden guilts and fears.
Time passed in quiet agony.

I pushed down the truth with a lie
like teardrops, or
a cut not yet healed.

How have you heart to kill the weak
your bitter words flowing like vinegar?
Am I really worth your time?

I won't cry for me.
What fruits will come from evil hate?
Fear is gone to pester another person.

Will you wilt, fold up, tuck away?
Life is short; don't waste it on a broken soul.
Share your voice before the world crumbles before us.

We are the ones.
We hold the key.
We are resilient.
Seize the moment.
People depend on us.
We must have ambition

Why must a dream be only a dream?
We WILL be the ones to make a difference in the world.
We speak of dreams, a future set free.

RUTH: In high school, bullying, cliques, and other problematic behaviors occur. How do you see your workshops helping teens change their behaviors such that they want to share leadership, stop bullying, or prevent bullying?

SARAH: The most obvious is tackling these topics head-on. We might spend a Saturday brainstorming contrasting qualities—those that bullies exhibit and those that would defuse bullying, for instance. We would then work in pairs to write scenarios that used both sets of qualities to understand how one might defuse the other. Or during the summer camp we redefined Barbies, each took on a positive persona. In the course of the week, the Barbies were renamed, redesigned, reclothed, and repurposed in stories where they encountered one another and worked together using their special powers to resolve real issues facing girls in their daily lives.

We did a similar process around leadership, personifying qualities the girls admired in strong female role models. I guess you might say the common core was a kind of role-playing through discussion and storytelling. Each would inform the other, a circle of learning where discussion prompted story, and story prompted more discussion. It was often in the sharing of these small-group-created stories that the larger group became most animated and opinionated. And I assure you, they had opinions *and* solutions for everything from bullying and body shaming to climate change and consumerism run amok. As an aside on the topic of leadership, I should mention that in addition to two adult leaders at each session, we also had one of the girls function as assistant. This gave her a taste of peer leadership. And several of the girls took these practices into school projects. I attended a number of presentations where many of our core practices clearly influenced their approach in designing their work.

Underlying all the experience is the simple fact that being heard deeply inspires self-confidence. The confidence these girls grew into was heartening beyond words. Of course it was not entirely because of Young Women Writing for (a) Change—not at all. But the girls who were drawn to our programs clearly had a desire to be change agents in their world.

RUTH: What kinds of areas of social change do you aim your work toward?

SARAH: We emphasize variations of "individual and social change" to refer to rebalancing the energies of individuals, families, and society to include the feminine more prominently in a culture that has become terribly skewed toward the extreme values of the masculine.

The concept of being a change agent within one's own life and the life of one's community seems almost inborn among the young women I have worked with. This new generation understands the extremes we have moved toward, manifest for instance in political polarity. They are concerned about the environment/Earth. They want to learn how to be better stewards of natural and social resources, their very future. Here are some examples:

> Dear Mother Earth (Gaia),
>
> I just wanted to say sorry. Not for anything I've done specifically, but for the harm that has befallen you in general. I wish I could say I actively pick up litter to help keep you clean, but that would be a lie. I do, however, strive to be someone you won't mind having to deal with.
>
> And I know that there are those out there who do much less than the little I do to help. The ones who throw away extra food that could have been composted, the ones who leave all their lights and TV on no matter if they're in the room or not, and the ones who toss plastic bags and wrappers out of their car windows. But even bigger than that are the owners of the industries. The recent oil spills? I am so sorry about that, Gaia. No one deserves that kind of treatment. I hope you believe in my sincerity. I want only the best for you, even though it can be hard to always remember.
>
> I'm sorry also for the lack of active help I've given you. And I want to say that I promise to do the best I can to always be conscious of you, and your needs and treatment. Tragically enough, there are so many people out there who aren't like that, and they should strive to be.
>
> I love nature. I really do. Two years ago, I asked for a tree for my birthday. We went to the nursery, picked out a cherry tree sapling, and planted it in our front yard. It will be two more years before it bears edible, ripe fruit, but for now I'm just happy with seeing all of its new growth.
>
> When I was little, I sang in a music group called the Minor Key. Even though I was little, I sang my own song titled "Earthkeeper." My favorite part goes, "choose to walk, not drive. Recycle my garbage, turn the heat down inside. Grow my own garden, reduce what I use. I am an Earthkeeper."
>
> So, Gaia, I will be an Earthkeeper, and this week and writing this letter has made me realize I don't do nearly as much as I could. I promise, here and now, to do only my best. Please trust that I will.
>
> Love, Nina (7/8/11)

They are concerned about bullying and its impact, as more and more young adults experience the loss of friends to suicide. They are concerned about the lack of mental health services for friends who are hurting, about homeless kids and economic inequality.

The girls write about taking leadership roles to make things better. They take on community projects to support local environmental stewardship; they volunteer at the food shelf. They are hungry for a just and peaceful world. They revel in natural beauty. They are themselves beautiful. Writing is an affirmation of their own uniqueness and strength. Sharing that writing models confidence to others.

### My Body

So strong, so real. My face, unblemished by unnatural material, untouched by the hands of the media. Full lips and almond-shaped eyes, dark brown. A nose with wide, flaring nostrils that move slightly as I breathe in and out. My arms, studded with muscles from years of martial arts, slender, brown, ready for work. Fine hair covers them, covers their gentle golden color, and thick hands, but graceful. Flitting over the strings of a cello or helping carry plates for the dinner table, my hands are graceful. Skin scarred from bug bites and scrapes stretched over strong, solid knuckles, and blue veins spring out daringly.

My legs flow from beneath my wide, curving hips. Hard, muscled, tense with energy as they sit folded on my chair, up to my chest. Scars cover the skin here too, scars of dog bites and jumping rope accidents, scars to be proud of, scars that add character to myself. Scars that are beautiful, just like the shape of my eyes, the color of my arms, and the veins of my hands. Beautiful like me.

Nina 7/6/11

### I Love My Body

A glance in the mirror is all it takes to hold me there. To make me appreciate how beautiful I am. I love all my features and when people compliment me, it doesn't matter, because I know perfectly well that my body is just that. Different, different because everyone is different. I smell clean and wonderful; my hair erupts with lovely scents when let down from its knot on the top of my head.

Delicious brown curls, corkscrews and waves, volume at its greatest. Stuck straight in the center of my olive face is my nose, what a little twitch at the end. And my fingers, as they close around the pen, or pencil, or book. Hands tough and callused to allow a firm grip, but soft and smooth to confirm a careful dance, hand in hand. On my feet, toenails teal, but not for long, as I must repaint them soon, bringing new charm. A curved arch comes with a bounce in my step, sprinting through wet grass on a humid night. The tree trunks sway as I stand tall against the scenery of fast moving traffic. All of these parts of me, they are mine. A glance in the mirror is all it takes.

Ellie 7/6/11

The poem that follows was created as a joint project by girls at a local summer day camp called Rosie's Girls. This is a trades exploration program that helps girls develop and strengthen their capacities and confidence while exposing them to a range of educational and career options they may never have considered. Girls entering grades 6 to 8 can try their hand at carpentry, welding, self-defense, and auto repair—challenging themselves and each other—while experiencing both leadership and teamwork in an atmosphere that is fun, supportive, and positive.

In July 2009, I offered a weekly writing circle to these girls. It was an incredibly moving experience. After a mere three sessions, the girls "got" the purpose of writing for personal reflection. They "got" the sense of how a strong community can be woven despite disparate backgrounds and experiences. They "got" the message that they are worthwhile and full of promise. And they "got" the power of words to express themselves.

The following poem was constructed on the spot during our third session. I read Nikki Giovanni's "Revolutionary Dreams" poem. Then each girl was asked to complete a sentence from the poem in as many ways as possible, thinking both big and small, in terms of both today and when they would be older. They were instructed to write at least three different things, one on each card, and to base their writing on things they experienced/learned about themselves/their abilities and interests during camp. I prompted them to think especially of times they took risks, made tough choices, overcame a challenge.

Once these lists were complete, the girls were given fifteen minutes to work in a group. They laid out all the cards, read them over, and decided together on ones that are either unique or universal. They were to select the six strongest lines.

Each group then laid out their six lines on a central table. The girls circled around, looking them over to make one poem about themselves based on who they were becoming out of this recent camp experience. The final poem was typed up and copied for each of them and was posted on the Vermont Works for Women and Women Writing for (a) Change—Vermont websites. Here it is:

**Rosie's Girls' Revolutionary Dream**

I will be the one to spread Rosies around the world,
who other girls, like I am now, look up to;
the one who creates world peace,
who helps others when they are in need,
helps the daughters and sons of the world,
the one to keep on learning every day all the time until I'm gone.

I will be the one who is brave and goes first on any challenge,
who takes care of my body so I may live longer;
the one to accept others, be interested in everyone's differences,
who isn't afraid to speak her mind and doesn't care what anyone else
thinks,
to stand strong for myself and accept myself for who I am.
I will be the one dancing around the fire singing to the moon (but I won't
be the only one.)

I will be the one who inspires and helps others to reach their potential,
who learns new skills, tries new things, builds new confidence all my life,
who provides for the people around me,
who builds my own house with all natural chemical-free materials.
I will be the one who looks inside and pulls herself out,
who learns to fly without wings.

I will be the one who isn't afraid to take risks to make my dreams come
true,
who always has plenty of patience with those around her,
who is blind to the color of skin,

push the barrier of the MLB to allow women,
become a professional soccer player.
I will be the one to become the first woman president.

I will be the one who helps change the difference between men and women to only physical things
who grows her own food, cooks it up and feeds her friends,
the one with dirt always under my fingernails,
who realizes that being yourself will get you farther in life than anything you can imagine.
I will be the one who can positively and confidently lead others,
the one who came with little dignity and left with it all.

To give you an idea of how powerful this experience was to the girls—in their own words—here is a sampling from thirty comments on final evaluation cards addressing *what I came here expecting; what I leave here owning*:

> I expected to learn about poems or writing and I left here owning the skills of a poem writer.
>
> When I first came to the writing class I thought "why are we doing writing?" Then it seemed to express ourselves and I grew to like it. Thanks!
>
> I came here expecting to write a lot. I leave owning an awakening imagination and a buzzing mind.
>
> What I came here expecting: a class where I had to write about boring things . . . What I left here owning: the ability to express myself better, through writing. ♥
>
> I didn't expect to think about writing that way. The poems kind of stuck throughout each session. It was much funner and thoughtful than I expected.
>
> I came expecting a boring writing sessions. I left owning . . . myself.
>
> I came here expecting to do schoolwork. I left owning words of strength.
>
> When I came to the writing course, I expected structure. I left with freedom, and the skill to empty my mind onto paper.
>
> Expecting: to have to write a bunch . . . Owning: what more feelings meant and you gave everyone a chance.

> I came here expecting boredom. I left owning dignity.
>
> I came here expecting to write about boring things and I am leaving with skills I did not have before.

RUTH: Artists often use words and something else; for example, words and music or words and movement. What is your lived experience in creating language and having that language brought to life by the use of another art form?

SARAH: In workshops, summer retreats, and monthly "art 'n writing evenings," I routinely offer what I call "cross training" experiences. Even inside the women's prison, we use art in conjunction with writing to deepen the insights that emerge through writing.

Whether we use Deborah Koff-Chapin's SoulCards as inspiration, create our own string-and-ink drawing that we later interpret and enhance, experiment with TouchDrawing, glue collage, or make meditative mandalas, the experience—both inside and out, with the girls and adults, on retreat or in focused workshops with sound or movement *and* writing—the fundamental experience is always the deepening of felt experience and self-knowledge through the weaving of expressive art and written language.

We start with a poem, take a line from the poem as a writing prompt, then move into the visual art with those ideas/feelings in mind, though not necessarily to "show" them in the art, just to have a framework. Music is usually involved. After a period of time—maybe forty-five minutes or an hour, depending on the art form—we generally look back at the art and reflect on it in different ways. If mandalas or collage, we will often "read" the images we have produced, coming back into our conscious minds to glean the wisdom or message the creation might have for us. The result is often a poem, and always a deepened understanding of some aspect of their being.

## *Snapshot*

### Suzanne Adams, Houston, Texas

*Workshop facilitator for adolescent girls, writer*

"It's All About You," a writing and expressive arts workshop for adolescent girls developed as part of my graduate work in TLA, is an eight-week program that focuses on encouraging and empowering girls in self-expression, identity, goal setting, and relationships. Over the last five years, I've facilitated the workshop in many venues, including public and private schools, afterschool programs, and county juvenile probation departments. To encourage writing as a TLA practice, each participant in the workshop receives a journal.

My own journal writing through the years has been an invaluable gift—a vessel for my voice, a fount of inspiration, an alchemical mystery that extracts wisdom from life's experiences. People talk about writing their hearts out, but I think I've spent hours and hours writing my heart in. I write as a personal TLA practice, while also writing fiction and nonfiction for a broader audience.

What I love about TLA is when we write about what matters most to us, our hands become a magic wand, transferring what lies deep within us into an insight or epiphany on the page. We discover and rediscover ourselves in unexpected, profound ways. TLA reminds us to follow the compass of our hearts and to listen to the voice in our souls. In the midst of all the noise and distractions around us, that compass is still and that voice is quiet. Can you hear it?

www.writetothecenter.com

# *Snapshot*

## Minna Dubin, San Francisco, California

*Workshop facilitator for women and youth, and writer*

I'm interested in empowering youth to bring their stories to a wider audience through journaling, memoir, monologue, and poetry. My work often ends in big final projects, such as a monologue show at a local theater or an art installation on the steps of the public library.

Since 2008, I've been running creative writing workshops for all types of young people. My focus on women and pregnant and parenting teens began with a project I did with young mothers and young writers in Lexington, Kentucky, and in San Francisco. Having just completed a three-year artist residency with San Francisco's WritersCorps, where I worked in a school for pregnant and parenting teens and at the Main Library, I'm currently spending time with my son, writing about the beautiful and relentless tornado of motherhood, and figuring out my next steps as an independent TLA practitioner.

When I share my writing and people respond, "That's my story!" I realize the power of our words. In working with teens over extended periods, I see them experience that buzz, and believe in themselves and their stories more. I love when the student who was always looking annoyed and staring at her phone under the table is thrilled to let her beautiful writing flow. This transformation is at its highest when my students perform. They realize the gravity of their words and the power they have.

www.minnadubin.com

# 5

# Zamlers, Tricksters, and Queers

## *Re-Mixing Histories in Yiddishland and Faerieland*

Ezra Berkley Nepon

> When the [culture-]creators are on the margins, archivists are activists; when materials are archived, they achieve the status of something significant enough to be worth saving, and then those artifacts are available so that scholars, students, and other activists may continue engaging with them.
>
> —*Alison Piepmeier,* Make Your Own History: Documenting Feminist and Queer Activism in the 21st Century *(2012, ix)*

We speak of transformative language arts as "a profoundly radical response to the fragmentation, isolation, violence, hopelessness, and despair of our culture," one that "brings people literally back to their roots, and from that perspective, gives them a wider view of what they and what their communities might be" (Transformative Language Arts Network, 2014). By telling our own stories, and through remembering, retelling, and rewriting our larger stories, we find new ways forward, repairing and regenerating our personal and cultural possibilities.

My own work has been an exploration of the ways that TLA practice can overlap with the field of "people's history"—history as told through the stories of regular people, including the understanding of social transformations as mass movements rather than individual hero narratives. Readers may be familiar with Howard Zinn's classic book *A People's History of the United*

*States*, which retells American history from 1492 to 2003, with a focus on social movements that created cultural shifts. People's history also overlaps broadly with the field of social history, which blossomed in 1960s and 1970s in the United States, including focus areas such as women's history, black history, and labor history, and continues to inform conversations about what counts as historically valuable.

As we tell our stories and the stories of our cultures, and as that communication brings us toward personal and social transformation, aren't we also doing the work of people's history? Aren't the stories we tell also a kind of archive? If we understand our own stories and storytelling as meaningfully part of a collective history, does that help us clarify how these stories can make change beyond the individual, catalyzing collective transformation?

I entered the Goddard College TLA MA program in 2011 with an intention to use elements of memoir, historical fiction, and magical realism as a route to those retellings. Instead, I found myself digging deeper into my love of radical history by researching and documenting two contemporary examples of political theater-makers who do this retelling work in their productions: a troupe, the Eggplant Faerie Players, and an individual, Jenny Romaine.

Through interviews, archival work, and my own experiences collaborating with Jenny Romaine and members of the Eggplant Faerie Players, I produced a document that functions as people's history; it puts their political and creative strategies on record in a new way. As the project progressed, the artists shared that the experience of having their decades of creative life and labor honored by documentation and critical engagement was an important element of the project's transformative impact. This work was also TLA-in-practice for me, as I wrote my way through to great clarity about why these artists' work has impacted me so deeply, and what it means for my own creative, scholarly, and personal life.

I was drawn to these artists because they have each cultivated thriving creative communities that are abundant in participation, cooperation, and imagination. The Eggplant Faerie Players performance troupe developed out of Radical Faerie culture and HIV/AIDS activism. Its style of irreverent satire blends ingredients, including clowning, camp, wordplay, and musical numbers. Located within a rural queer artist community in middle Tennessee called Idyll Dandy Arts (IDA), the Eggplant Faerie Players have been touring shows, including *Person Livid with AIDS*, *Next Year in Sodom*, and *Welcome to Homo Holler*, since the late 1980s—shows that serve as a kind of archive of their queer subculture over the decades. The Eggplant Faerie Players talk about serious politics in ridiculous outfits from Appalachia to Amsterdam.

Jenny Romaine is a theater-maker in New York City whose specific brand of "ethnographic surrealism" re-mixes Yiddish archival source material with ongoing cultural exploration to produce avant-garde "New Yiddish Theater." Her methodology is informed by growing up in secular Yiddish Leftist culture, studying folklore and performance studies, learning pageantry skills with Bread and Puppet and the Ninth Street Theater, and then working in the YIVO (Yiddish culture) sound archive for thirteen years. She is a founding member of Great Small Works theater collective and longtime bandleader of Circus Amok. Jenny is also the director of Jews for Racial and Economic Justice's annual Purimshpil as well as The Sukkos Mob, the KlezKamp Youth Theater Workshop, and of many more productions of theater, street protest, and other spectacles.

## Re-Arranging the Fragments, Documenting the Margins

In many marginalized communities, certainly including the LGBT and Jewish communities that these artists are rooted in, segments of the community push for assimilation into mainstream culture in hopes that blending in will make the community safer, stronger, less vulnerable. In contrast, Jenny Romaine and the Eggplant Faerie Players are aggressively anti-assimilation. They critique mainstream culture, calling for radical change. They dig deep into their cultural roots, not frozen in nostalgia but instead Re-Mixing History into a regenerating, evolving, vital radical culture. They demand the right to dialogue with their traditions, proclaiming that fundamentalist and orthodox communities—those with conservative and nostalgic relationships to the traditions—don't own the legacy.

Because of their anti-assimilationist politics, and their challenges to capitalism and business as usual, these artists' work is not commercially viable and therefore may not be seen as "valuable" in mainstream culture. When they find openings to reach wider audiences there is a sense of "getting away with it"—getting away with subversive political agitation. This is part of their strength, but it also results in their decades of work being underdocumented.

As a historian—as someone offering stories and critical analysis about marginalized cultures—I'm interested in how these histories are archived, remembered, represented, and performed. I was especially engaged by questions about what happens when researchers from marginalized cultures research and write about our own communities, or those we descend from. Although there are certainly ethical concerns to be attended to, I was excited by the opportunities—the possibility of honoring parts of our culture that go unseen, or even purposely hidden, when viewed from outside. How do we move beyond invisibility, nostalgia, or objectification to build new liberatory culture from our people's histories? These questions apply both to my own research, writing, and theorizing and to how the artists I document here respond to the same questions in their creative work.

I had a sense that the stories of the Eggplant Faerie Players and Jenny Romaine were important to document in their own right. As my research deepened, I saw that I could easily write a book about either of them, but I suspected that another dimension of meaning would emerge from looking at the stories together. I was also coming to understand that Jenny Romaine's theatrical methodology—ethnographic surrealism—refers to a way of making art from fragments of our cultural history. By re-arranging the fragments, new culture, new learning, and new opportunities manifest. In writing profiles of Jenny Romaine and the Eggplant Faerie Players, I was collecting the fragments of their creative ethnographies. How could I re-mix these fragments, practicing this methodology in my own work? I realized that I needed to not only put the pieces of the stories in a metaphorical room together, but also to bring the artists together themselves.

In October 2012, Jenny Romaine and I traveled to Idyll Dandy Arts in Tennessee to spend a weekend talking and learning together with the Eggplant Faerie Players. That weekend, I interviewed Jenny and Eggplant Faeries SPREE and MaxZine. I also held a group interview with Eggplant Faeries TomFoolery, Leopard Zeppard, Sandor Katz, Dashboard, and Junebug, with MaxZine zipping in and out while collecting garden ingredients for dinner. Now, these interviews don't reflect the optimal sound quality situation I might hope for in an oral history interview. Many of these conversations were recorded outdoors with background noise of a running stream, birds, people walking by. The group interview is a frenetic and hilarious conversation between a group of friends/housemates/neighbors/collaborators of twenty years around a kitchen table, while more friends and neighbors cook a massive feast a few feet away. Audibly, it is total chaos, and it beautifully reflects the joy, collectivism, and humor of Faerieland.

In addition to my own interviews, I drew heavily from interviews with MaxZine, SPREE, Sandor, and Dashboard conducted by the ACT UP Oral History Project. Interviews with Jenny Romaine also came from the Yiddish Book Center's Wexler Oral History Project and radio programs, including NYC's "Beyond the Pale" (WBAI) and Montreal's "Shtetl on the Shortwave" (CKUT). I looked through two decades of *Radical Faerie Digest* quarterly journals at the William Way LGBT Center archives in Philadelphia, where I found a number of articles written by the Eggplant Faerie Players. I also used the personal performance archives of the artists, with their permission, and was able to digitize a number of Eggplant Faerie Player performances from VHS and Hi-8 tapes with the help of a small grant from a Radical Faerie arts organization whose funding cycle was entitled "Through the Past, A Queerer Tomorrow, Today."

I offer these research-method details in part to identify the ways in which, though I was informed by scholarly conversations about anthropology and social history, these profiles draw directly from the artists' own stories, with questions asked and answered in the context of their own communities. Gathering these details of the artists' lives and creative works was a process that reminded me of that undertaken by the volunteer zamlers—collectors—of Eastern European Jewish folk culture in the period before World War II. I think the powerful story of these zamlers can offer insight into the overlap between people's history, archives of our everyday lives, and the work of transformative language arts.

## On Zamlers and Chickens in Revolt

YIVO (Yidisher Visnshaftlekher Institut) was founded in 1925 by scholars in Vilnius and Berlin with the mission of documenting the Yiddish culture of

Eastern Europe. YIVO came out of an interwar movement that talked about *doikayt* (hereness)—a commitment to Jewish survival where they were (Eastern Europe), as opposed to many who were leaving with the (pre-state) Zionist movement or the promise of a better life in America. The YIVO archive project was a response to big questions about how to build an economically viable life in Europe, and how to build a sense of possibility despite being brutally oppressed at a structural level. "A virtual cult of documentary collection existed in Jewish Eastern Europe between 1925 and 1939, with the Vilna YIVO as its temple," writes David E. Fishman in *The Rise of Modern Yiddish Culture* (2005, 141). "Groups of volunteer zamlers in scores of cities and towns in Poland, Lithuania, Romania, and across the globe inundated YIVO with a mass of historical, literary, artistic, and ethnographic materials." Jenny Romaine reflected on the work of the zamlers:

> They saw that Jews had this amazing culture. Every melody, every kehila [community], every newspaper, every traditional practice was on the plus side of their power economy. They asked, "As an ethnic disenfranchised, despised minority, how can we live here and make it work? We have all this stuff, what can we do? First we have to know who the youth are, and we have to let them know that who they are is important to us." They did autobiography contests for the youth, collecting these incredible stories of what people were enduring. They also went out to all the shtetlach [small Jewish towns], and they zogt [said], "sing me every melody you know," and they recorded it. They went and took all the record books from the Jewish communities. These [archivists] saw that in every aspect of religious life and traditional life—in the foodways, and you name it—there is information to be transmitted, and that this was a cultural powerbank. And they said that it's going be through the rearrangement of these fragments, that we create something new.
>
> (Kramer, 2010)

In the language of today's movement building, YIVO created an asset-based organizing campaign—the strategy of starting with recognition of what you already have in abundance, and using those strengths to build power.

In 1941, the Nazis occupied Vilnius and killed most of the YIVO community, transferring some of the collection to a center for the documentation of Jewish extinction, and destroying the rest. A group of Jews assigned to sort the Nazi collection, "the Paper Brigade," defiantly hid what they could in secret locations in the Vilne ghetto—within the floors and walls and buried underground. After World War II, a few members of the Paper Brigade returned—survivors who had valiantly escaped the death camps and made it through the war hidden in forests, fighting for their lives. There was a dedicated effort by survivors and researchers to reclaim hidden archival documents, including documentation of the horrors of the ghettos and concentration camps that had been hidden away by resistance groups like the Paper Brigade in Vilnius and the Oyneg Shades group in Warsaw. After the fall of the Nazis, the materials that were saved were once again endangered and partially destroyed under Stalinism, with another underground rescue mission established to spirit what could be carried out to America. While only a fraction of the massive original collection was saved, it was a basis for rebuilding a major archive in NYC. Today, the YIVO collection holds more than 24 million items, including books, documents, recordings, photographs, and other artifacts (YIVO, 2014).

Jenny Romaine worked intimately with the sound archive of Yiddish European life, including a major shipment of newly discovered materials that had been hidden in Vilnius. She remembers that when they opened these boxes, everyone wept because the people who had created the archives were all gone (Kramer, 2010). It was in this work that she started to develop a sense of the importance of fragments.

The ethnographic archive of Eastern European Jewry is necessarily fragmented because of a legacy of repression, oppression, and genocide. The fragments that the YIVO researchers and the many volunteer collectors gathered amidst anti-Jewish policies and pogroms, and then what survived the destruction of Nazism and Stalinism are what remain of the "cultural powerbank." In a daily way, Jenny was working with the fragments of the Yiddish cultural legacy, and she came to see that she could work with those pieces through her artistic practice—re-arranging, layering, and montaging them—Re-Mixing History to build new culture.

So, what does all this actually look like in Jenny's "New Yiddish Theater" productions? The Nekhame Epshteyn Chicken Park is one example of how the YIVO archive fragments are re-arranged in Jenny's shows. In the summer of 2011, the KlezKanada [annual Yiddish Culture gathering outside of Montreal] theme was "Humor." Jenny wanted to focus on a woman because "there are so many women that are invisible to us." Yiddish scholar

Itzik Gottesman provided inspiration, telling Jenny about a woman named Nekhame Epshteyn, a YIVO researcher who had collected and catalogued ten thousand Yiddish jokes!

Epshteyn was a poet, translator, and teacher in the secular Yiddish schools in Vilnius, and a key member of the Ethnographic Folklore Commission that fed into YIVO. Focused on jokes, she classified her collection by both their "garb" ("the environment around the persons") and their "goal" ("what were they really laughing at"). Epshteyn escaped from the Vilne ghetto when the Germans occupied Lithuania, but she was caught and killed in the 1942 Ponar massacre (Gottesman, 2003, 159).

Jenny dug into Epshteyn's files in the YIVO archive to learn a bunch of jokes. That summer at KlezKanada, the Nekhame Epshteyn Chicken Park was born, using a portable amusement park run by chickens as a frame to teach about Yiddish ethnography from the nineteenth and early twentieth century through the story of Epshteyn and her Yiddish jokes. The props included fifteen flat chickens, eight intricate life-size marionette chickens, all the enclosures for the amusement park areas, and a giant chicken puppet—15 feet tall. At a bar in the amusement park, the chickens told jokes about drinking. At a cemetery, chickens told cemetery jokes. You could go to a clairvoyant chicken. You could meet Epshteyn herself (chicken version) and tell her a joke of your own in her sound booth—if it was funny, a chicken would shoot out of a cannon.

Nekhame Epshteyn was murdered by fascists and rendered invisible by the destruction of the culture she was building and documenting. Through this show, hundreds of people learned of her name and her work, enabling us to honor and recover her legacy and to build new worlds (even portable amusement-park worlds) based on her creative vision. But Epshteyn's legacy wasn't the only political issue at stake in the park. As tour guide Jenny Romaine explained to the KlezKanada crowds: the park was not staffed but run by chicken labor. There were some employment issues arising. Things were a little tense. It was foreshadowing: the chickens were going to revolt.

A few months later, the chickens were back in action. Jenny and her band of performers paraded through a Brooklyn neighborhood street festival using street theater to tell a story using Jewish New Year themes and rituals. The show was woven through with gorgeous traditional music: "Avinu Malkeinu," a haunting prayer-song beseeching God to grant us justice and salvation, and a re-mixed version of "Yigdal," the hymn sung at the end of the

New Year's service. Nekhame Epshteyn's chickens were the central characters for the show, with a plot focused on the Hasidic ritual of "shluggin kapores" in which a chicken is swung overhead while a prayer is recited, asking that the sins of the Jews be driven into the chicken, and then the chicken is killed and fed to the poor. In this show, we learn that the chickens of Brooklyn are not happy. Jenny explains, "Imagine what it's like when your job description is to be killed and eaten for someone else's misconduct!" She continues, "To me the metaphor of the shluggin kapores was that the chickens are saying, 'F--- you, Wall Street! We're not gonna take this austerity that you're shoving down our throats. We're not gonna die for your sins.'"

We learn that the chickens' anxiety can erupt into compulsive joke-telling, and we hear a bunch of great jokes. Suddenly, a giant chicken shows up, and we learn that "the Chickens of Brooklyn are liberating themselves using advanced musical theater techniques!" We sing the traditional song "Mene Tekel U-Pharson," and out of the giant chicken comes a message—a translation of the song: "Your days are numbered, You've been weighed in the balance and found wanting. Your empire will fall. Your goose is cooked!" The chickens demand action on their unemployment woes. The crowd pledges, "Monster Chicken of misfires! We promise to interrupt our normal behavior! And to be continuously revolting!"

Just a few days after this performance on the streets of Brooklyn, the chickens (and their puppeteers) joined the ranks of a new social movement erupting in Manhattan—marching, chanting, and performing among the crowds at Occupy Wall Street. For those witnessing the performances, Nekhame Epshteyn's joke-telling chickens functioned as kind of mascot—performative representation of resistance to the 1 percent: a worker's movement that refuses to suffer for the sins of those more powerful. The chickens may have a sense of humor, but they're serious about resistance.

## Trickster Truth-Telling Queens

While Jenny expresses her connection to the archive of Jewish culture very clearly, the Eggplant Faerie Players talk less explicitly about the queer traditions from which they draw. Still, their trickster nature, their love of wordplay, and their references to the role of the "sacred clown" all demonstrate roots in this history. Judy Grahn (1984) explains the radical role of faeries and drag queens in her book *Another Mother Tongue*, which explores the origins of gay culture:

> Sensual, barbed, informative, revolting, political—Fairy speech is a living art . . . The drag queen is like the king's jester without the king, some theatrical combination of the Fool, the Hanged Man, and the Empress all rolled into one and without a true territory . . . Their usual character of speech is a spewing of a running stream of advice, predictions, protection, commentary, gossip, "truth-saying" (1984, 87). . . . And using the ancient chaotic powers, Gay trickster queens of all descriptions keep the matrix of human thought in the disrupted, tumultuous state that prevents stagnation and keeps true creativity and flexibility possible. (231)

The Eggplant Faerie Players' methods certainly reach back to queer histories, but their shows tend to serve primarily as (campy, satirical) zamler archives of their own subcultural lives and experiences. Troupe co-founder SPREE's performance in the show *Person Livid with AIDS* is a clear example of how theater served as a space for both documenting, reinterpreting, and transforming her own story of living with AIDS.

In 1995, while on tour with the show *Swishing Channels*, SPREE was putting on makeup when she noticed a lesion on her eyelid, and then one between her toes. She told MaxZine she thought she had Kaposi's sarcoma (KS), an AIDS-associated opportunistic infection. SPREE got the runaround from doctors, who told her first that she simply had an eyelid bruise and a fungus between her toes, then that she had syphilis. Back in Tennessee, she finally got a diagnosis of KS, but not before jumping through outrageous hoops to get health-care benefits covered through the state's "Tenn-Care" health benefit program. SPREE almost died of AIDS in 1996, but she lived just long enough to be pulled back from the brink by the new treatment option of protease inhibitors. She went on Norvir (ritonavir), a brand-new medication that was later used as part of a combination therapy (or "cocktail"). As one of the earliest users of this drug, she took it as a monotherapy. SPREE started to get better, but she also became extremely manic. It turned out that you weren't supposed to take the antidepressant drug Paxil with Norvir, but it was so new that her doctor didn't catch that interaction detail. Her body was flooded with serotonin, and she had what she "fondly refers to as a meltdown" that led to hospitalization in a Nashville psych ward. SPREE processed these experiences through theater in a way that offered her and her friends an outlet for personal catharsis of their traumatic experiences. At the same time, her show provided education to a broader community in the U.S. South at a time when few were exposed to the personal and political struggles of those living with the virus.

At first SPREE wanted to do a production of her friend Michael Smith's play *Person Livid with AIDS*. Smith had ended his life after a succession of AIDS-related hospitalizations, and SPREE wanted to get a script or tape of his show, but she couldn't track down a copy. In our interview she explained, "I kept trying and trying. And finally MaxZine said to me, 'Well, why don't you just do your own story. You've been through so much now that you could be the person livid with AIDS.' So it was my story and not Michael Smith's story that was the one that we did."

In putting the pieces back together, SPREE reclaimed power over her own past, present, and future. She re-mixed her own history, salvaging pieces of her story that were fragmented by her traumatic illness and mental health crisis, weaving them in with old and new performance pieces from the Eggplant Faerie Player collection.

The Eggplant Faerie Players opened their version of *Person Livid with AIDS* at the Dark Horse Theater in Nashville and then toured the show throughout the South. The show opens in darkness with the voices of cast members singing a medley of children's songs with lyrics rewritten to be about AIDS. Lights up on SPREE, sitting center stage in the wheelchair she had used during her increasing illness, but no longer needed. SPREE looks eerie, sort of frozen, but her eyes move back and forth dramatically. Finally she says:

> All right Mr. DeMille, I'm ready for my close up. Norma Desmond, this is your life. No, wait a minute, stop the tape! Stop, rewind, back up! That's not what this is at all. This isn't even "Gloria Swanson, this is your life." This is supposed to be "SPREE, this is your life." Oh, well, then in that case—all right, Mr. DeMille, I'm ready for my tap dance.
>
> [Tap Dances while saying:] Hello everybody, my name's SPREE! What's yours?
>
> [Finishes dancing:] And that on feet that had the lesions radiated off of them, thank you very much!

From her chair, SPREE tells her story: about working at the National AIDS Hotline, getting overwhelmed by losing so many friends and loved ones to AIDS, testing positive, having to jump through ridiculous hoops to access treatment, and her experience finally getting on the protease inhibitors and having a mental breakdown. Throughout this retelling, skits and song-and-dance interludes theatrically illuminate the story.

SPREE's classic character Barbara Broadcast tells hilarious tales of calls to the AIDS hotline, with a bevy of fancy queers kibitzing on phones behind her. Then SPREE does an onstage outfit change to become character R J Sneevely, who runs a condom recycling factory. In the original play, Michael Smith performed an imagined confrontation with a Canadian member of Parliament, taking off all his clothes and showing his KS lesions, saying to the MP: "Look at me, look at my body, I am a person livid with AIDS." SPREE remembers that was using the "anger" definition of livid, but when she looked up the word in Merriam-Webster Dictionary, she was amazed to find that the first definition of "livid" is "discolored by bruising: black-and-blue."

In the Eggplant Faerie Player show, Dashboard jumps up from the audience wearing a "FIGHT AIDS NOT ARABS" T-shirt and interrupts the condom recycling factory skit, starting the following dialogue:

> Dashboard: Stop the show! This wasn't livid. This was funny, it was humorous but it wasn't livid. What happened to outrage? What happened to fury? What happened to external manifestation of internal conflict projected on individuals and institutions in positions of power and authority? What happened to anger!
>
> SPREE: [Explains about the bruise definition of livid, lifts her shirt to show her KS lesions, then:] I am a person livid with AIDS, get it? And if I happen to think that humor is a good way of dealing with this epidemic or pandemic or whatever you want to call it, then so be it!

And there you have it: SPREE gets to define the terms of her own story. Dashboard gets to define his terms too—vocalizing his need for an outlet for his rage and powerlessness. This theatrical intervention allows the Players to dramatize a real struggle—the need for space for authentic, complex responses to trauma. This documentation of both humor and rage as responses to injustice is also a rejection of mainstream narratives of HIV+ people as passive victims.

As the show continues, SPREE tells of the outrageous barriers she faced in seeking competent medical care. Even despite being an ACT UP activist, an information specialist with the AIDS Hotline, and having a friend who worked at the Centers for Disease Control, the layers of Catch-22 drama she had to deal with are exhausting to recount. Finally, she calls in her friends to help her, and they do a fabulous musical clowning number called the "Tenn-Care Shuffle."

In the creative process of building the show, it evolved into a group production with a dozen people involved in writing and performing numbers. At some point, the group moved in a different direction than SPREE originally wanted. She'd come up with a vision of herself as a teacher, telling the school children about A-I-D-S and going into long strings of wordplay. Some of that initial monologue about letters, words, and sign language made it into the first part of the show, but the group didn't support her doing the full scene she envisioned. She was faced with a lack of control over her own story, and again she put the process into the show—documenting the conflict. From our interview:

> SPREE: Finally I just stand up out of my wheelchair and go, "wait a minute! that's not how it really happened!" and then I was like "this is my story!"
>
> Q: You put that process in the show?
>
> SPREE: Yeah, in the show I said, "you're telling this out of order, this is wrong, this is not the way that it happened. First this happened and then this happened and then I had a breakdown." And then I re-enacted the breakdown.
>
> JENNY: Was there any, what they call, catharsis?
>
> SPREE: Oh, sure, yes, oh, definitely. That's why I was doing it, to let it go and give it back out to the universe and hopefully educate some people.

In this show, SPREE and the Eggplant Faerie Players created an archive of the emotional and logistical details of life in their queer subculture during a time of both profound trauma and fast-paced change. With this production, they proclaim that their stories and their voices matter and must be heard on their own terms. They resist being rendered invisible, regenerating their community's power and possibility.

## Where to from Here?

We often associate the practice of TLA with workshops and other spaces where people gather to write and share our stories. A workshop I facilitated at the TLA Network's 2012 Power of Words conference may offer some helpful ideas about exploring the connection to people's history in these forums.

In "TLA & People's History," participants, heretofore referenced as "we," started an exercise based on mapping Venn diagrams—interlocking circles—about the larger histories that connect to our own stories. This might include geographic histories, cultural, gendered, ethnic, religious, class histories, as well as the social movements or transformative moments we've intersected with. First we made maps of what our history diagram looked like ten years ago, then a map based on our current lives, then imagined what our maps will look like ten years from now. This offered a space to think about the trajectories, commonalities, and shifts in the larger social histories our stories overlap with. We talked about what we saw and what we learned in the process.

This exercise generated a lot of ideas. One participant, Femmy, noted that at first we thought about the histories connected to identities (i.e., queer white people living in the South), then histories connected to interests (farming, theater), and then the histories around epistemology (what we've been learning/reading/thinking about). Femmy asked, "What would this exercise look like if we did a yearly circle? When did new areas appear? What 'sector' do new ways of being emerge in?"

When workshops bring ordinary people together to write about our lives, we are also documenting our histories, being zamlers, creating our own archives. How and when do these shared stories move beyond personal transformation and into larger social transformations? What are the models of TLA work that take our stories and bridge them into collective change? One of the themes that emerged from this workshop, and from my profiles of the Eggplant Faerie Players and Jenny Romaine, is the idea that writing down our stories is only one step in the transformation process. What comes next is another crucial step: sharing our stories with others. Whether that comes in the form of reading something out loud in a group, producing a traveling performance, or publishing a poem—it's the point at which our work is out in the world mixing and re-mixing with the other cultural fragments that we break out of isolation to receive new information about our connection to the collective, opening us up to imagine new paths.

## References

Eggplant Faerie Players. 1996. *Person livid with AIDS*. VHS.

Fishman, David E. 2005. *The rise of modern Yiddish culture*. Pittsburgh, PA: University of Pittsburgh Press.

Gottesman, Itzik Nakhmen. 2003. *Defining the Yiddish nation: The Jewish folklorists of Poland*. Detroit: Wayne State University Press.

Grahn, Judy. 1984. *Another mother tongue: Gay words, gay worlds*. Boston: Beacon.

Kramer, Tamara. Interview with Jenny Romaine. "Shtetl on the Shortwave." CKUT, 90.3 FM, March 5, 2010.

Piepmeier, Alison, 2012. Archives as activism: A preface. In *Make your own history: Documenting feminist and queer activism in the 21st century*, eds. Lyz Bly and Kelly Wooten. Los Angeles: Litwin.

Transformative Language Arts Network. 2014. What is Transformative Language Arts? http://www.tlanetwork.org/about/what-is-tlan/ (accessed February 5, 2014).

YIVO Institute for Jewish Research. 2014. Brief introduction. http://www.yivo institute.org/about/ (accessed February 5, 2014).

## *Snapshot*

### Miriam Gabriel, Orlando, Florida, and Long Island, New York

*Blogger and spoken-word artist*

A transformative pursuit, and performance, of language permeates my life. Most days, my fingers are occupied writing academic essays, poems, and performance slams/songs. Recently, I have been finding myself typing across the new territory of blog-writing, stemming from an increasing appreciation for the global intimacy of doing art in cyberspace.

I currently blog for the Transformative Language Arts Network, Reality Sandwich, and Evolutionary Landscapes. I also moderate learning sessions at the Evolver Intensives, focusing my input on a perpetual democratization of academic knowledge and championing of the imagination as a way of knowing.

For the past five years, I have been reciting poems at coffee shops and socially conscious gatherings in New York City and Orlando, Florida, exploring feminist intimacy and socially engaged spirituality. I've led workshops on intuitive research and Sufi-influenced activism for the past two years. In addition, I translate stories online between artists and activists across Egypt and the United States.

None of these projects would have ever emerged without the daily practice of intimate, written communication, in person and online. I'm propelled most by creating in community, via interviews and performances. When alone, I *love* the feeling of slow-simmering a poem like a meal, digesting the words in community, exhaling full-bellied together. TLA is not just artistic or therapeutic, it is also theoretical, active, critically reflective, and creatively connective with the visceral and the potential in another living being's life.

www.mirigabriel.com

## Snapshot

### Ruth Gendler, Berkeley, California

*Writer, artist, and facilitator of workshops for children and adults*

I am drawn to language that is rooted in heart and hand, eyes and feet, body and soul, sound and silence. Like the breath, language moves in and through and around us. Writing invites us to go inside and come out with something new. It often requires us to slow down and to listen to words that are little more than whispers, to listen with an outer ear to the sounds of water and wind, birds and traffic, to listen with an inner ear to the longings, laments, and songs of our own and others' hearts and souls.

Writing together in small groups can be an act of reverence, response, dialogue with the world. I teach writing workshops in a variety of settings: as a poet in the school, in private workshops for adults and children, and working with people one-to-one. I am especially excited about a monthly writing and art workshop for children and a writing workshop for artists at various galleries. Many artists have been scared away from writing (just as many of us have been scared away from drawing and painting), and I find that the writing that artists do can be delightfully precise and playful.

I am the author of three books of "lyrical nonfiction," which include my artwork. *Notes on the Need for Beauty: An Intimate Look at This Essential Quality* (Da Capo, 2007) celebrates beauty as a pathway that travels between the senses and the soul. Beauty connects the intimate aspects of our lives with the immense world we live in. We find beauty in the small garden outside the back door and the majestic redwood grove, the humble and the majestic. Writing my way into a deeper understanding of the wisdom of beauty gave me greater respect for many layers and stages of creative process. As I glimpsed what wanted to be said and grew into the person who could say it,

I gained a patience that seems very foreign to our quickening culture. I also discovered I have written my way deeper into making art.

*The Book of Qualities* (HarperCollins, 1988) personified seventy-six emotional attributes in brief paragraphs. Now in its fifty-fifth printing, *Qualities* has been adapted for theater and dance, translated into German, Japanese, Spanish, and Chinese, quoted in speeches and sermons, and featured in literary, psychological, and educational publications. I was the editor and illustrator for the anthology of poetry and prose, *Changing Light: The Eternal Cycle of Night and Day* (HarperCollins, 1991).

Often my artwork precedes and opens the way to my writing. Art continually deepens my experience, challenges me to deal with the physical world, and offers a contrast to the sequential lines of language. Most recently I have been working on a group of prints and paintings called "Peace Prayers" and preparing an exhibit of children's picture poems that I hope to make into a book.

I love seeing and hearing the vastness of our imaginations, working with language and image, feeling and meaning. I love that what we work on works on us.

www.ruthgendler.com

6

# Performing for Social Change

## Interviews with Kao Kue, Taína Asili, and Katt Lissard

RUTH FARMER

Over the winter holidays, I talked with three artists about using performance as a catalyst for social change and their thoughts about the transformative language arts field. Kao Kue is a Philadelphia-based Hmong spoken-word performer, poet, storyteller, and teacher. Taína Asili is an internationally acclaimed singer-songwriter who also facilitates social change workshops. Katt Lissard is a Goddard College faculty member, artistic director of the international Winter/Summer Institute, and a Fulbright Scholar. The women's primary art forms are very different—spoken word, singing, and theater. However, they all use these forms as ways to foster communication among communities about pressing social issues, ranging from police brutality to prison reform to HIV/AIDs.

## Kao Kue: Spoken-Word Artist of Hmong Traditions

RUTH: When you think of transformative language arts, what comes to mind?

KAO: Although the terminology "transformative language arts" is a more modern term, the philosophy and ideology behind the term is as old as humankind. I think back to the first pioneers and inventors in human civilization, and how they were able to turn sound into song, poetry, and story in order to connect to each other. Today, transformative artists continue to use the arts to connect community members to each other. In particular, I am happy to see young Hmong American artists connecting different generations of Hmong Americans together. Spoken-word artists, such as Tou Saiko Lee, are integrating traditional Hmong folk arts with hip-hop and other popular art forms to tell the experiences of the Hmong American community and history. I see the continuity of the generations of artists using their creativity to challenge injustices and create spaces for unity and harmony.

RUTH: Tell me what your current profession is.

KAO: Teaching at a charter school, K–8; third and fourth graders, the Folk Arts Cultural Treasure Charter School (FACTS). This school is about eight or nine years old. It is relatively small. Two classes per grade. The school offers a folk art residency, African drumming, Indonesian dance, mandala residency. I offer ESL support. FACTS was founded in 2005 by Asian Americans United, the Philadelphia Folklore Project, and other community organizers to address the educational disparity in the Asian and immigrant communities in Philadelphia. The school's mission is to provide a rigorous academic curriculum as well as expose our students and their families to different folk arts. Our school offers different residencies throughout the year (Tibetan mandala, Vietnamese Dan Tranh, Step, Chinese Opera, Chinese Lion Dance and Drumming, Indonesian Dance, Spoken Word, Liberian Storytelling, African Dance and Drumming, Chinese puppetry).

My job is mainly to provide language support and instruction for English-language learners, but the school's collaborative teaching model has allowed me to teach many content areas to the entire class (social studies, reading, writing, science). I have worked with grades K–8 and have infused poetry, storytelling, and song in many of my lessons. I have learned that the arts engage students and help them express themselves in a more unrestricted way. For example, when introducing adjectives, I have had my students act out these traits. Acting helps them to visualize and embody meanings of these words.

Poetry and music have always been in my life, especially since it was such an intimate part of my grandparents' and parents' lives. Through my grandparents and parents, I've learned that poetry and song are natural parts of me. It has brought me so much joy to incorporate more song and poetry into the teaching profession. I do this because I want poetry and song to be a part of my students' lives also.

RUTH: Tell us about the ways in which poetry is part of your grandparents' and parents' lives.

KAO: Culturally, singing and storytelling were a natural part of my parents and grandparents. They embodied their arts. I remember my grandmother cooking and singing all the time. She would also just sit down and tell us stories. When I interviewed my parents about folk art, they told me that was their main source of entertainment. Folk art is what they did and who they were.

Today, for people to sit around telling traditional stories is unusual. Being first-generation Hmong, my grandparents embodied what TLA was. It was a normal kind of thing we experienced, growing up listening and watching our parents and grandparents sing songs, tell stories, or play Hmong traditional instruments. I feel a great sense of loss now in second-generation Hmong. We are tending to lean toward electronics. We don't sit around talking to each other as a family as we used to do. This disappearance of the folk arts in the Hmong American community was a part of the reason for me to learn more about Hmong traditional arts. I began to interview my parents and elders to learn about Hmong arts and history.

Aside from learning about Hmong arts, I have created stories and performance pieces that infuse my Hmong and American heritages. I have also enjoyed performing poetry and song in the community and feel it is a vital source of spiritual and creative energy for me. Whether I am singing at a senior center or performing spoken word for high school youths, it has been so empowering to use the arts to converse with many different peoples. I believe the arts can break down barriers and build bridges for different communities to come together.

RUTH: Do you work with seniors and youth regularly?

KAO: Once a month with the Asian Arts Initiative, working with youth. I go there to support a friend who leads a workshop. I also volunteer occasionally at a senior center. I visit them and help them write and edit their stories. There was a senior writing project called "The Best Day of My Life So Far" that I got involved in a couple years ago. The project includes young professionals and youth volunteers who collect the senior stories and post them onto The Best Day of My Life So Far blog. This connects seniors to technologies and the Internet.

I feel I am my most genuine and true self when I am performing. I haven't turned my art into a paid profession; however, I am looking for ways to use the arts in my everyday life. Whether it is teaching youth or collaborating with other artists to perform poetry and song in community centers, I know that I need the arts in my life. I couldn't address the complex issues of intergenerational trauma, violence, racism, and sexism without my poetry and storytelling.

It has been difficult to live as a transformative artist because the arts are so undervalued in society today, but I have placed my faith in my art. I have learned that eventually poetry and song create opportunities when I do not know how to overcome pain and disappointment. For example, I have been able to use poetry and song to help my coworkers talk about their experiences of racism and to examine their own biases. It wasn't easy for me to address some of my coworkers who were resentful and defensive about this professional development topic. I found strength through singing and storytelling during each session. Together, my coworkers and I are working to build trust and to challenge our own biases for our students.

RUTH: How did you convince your coworkers to use singing and poetry as part of professional development?

KAO: It wasn't a matter of trying to convince anybody. Because of our mission, FACTS is supportive of the arts in our curriculum and professional development. We've had faculty choir and things like that since the school started. When I told the antibias committee I wanted to contribute my singing and storytelling, my coworkers and the school administrators gave me the space. I said, "I think I'm going to sing right now. Is that okay?" and they would say, "Sure." They were very supportive.

RUTH: It seems to me that you *are* being paid as a transformative language artist, in some ways.

KAO: Not in a direct way. It just happened organically. Because song and poetry are such a natural part of me, I perform art instinctively. For example, when the shooting in [Newtown] Connecticut happened, FACTS staff had a meeting about our school security. The acting principal asked me to sing. The staff knew I liked to sing, and so I knew I had to contribute my voice to the community during these troubled times.

RUTH: Would you share the lyrics to a song that you used to make transition to deeper discussions with coworkers or community members?

KAO: I have sung a few Hmong folk songs. Here is an example, roughly translated:

The earth sways and erupts
With the approach of Warfare
We do not want to leave our homes,
But we follow our elders to foreign lands
We enter the strangers' house
I till and slave for foreigners
Wondering if it will take
A lifetime to repay my gratitude.
Although we have left our homelands
Only to meet with this fate
Let us not turn tiger
Wearing stripes at our darkest hour
Let us have hope that one day
Our elders will take us
Back to the place of our birth

RUTH: That's a beautiful choice for deepening dialogue. How do you determine what positive social change is? What kinds/areas of social change do you aim your work toward?

KAO: I try to be genuine, and I hope that my storytelling is contributing to the community. An important part of my storytelling involves the empowerment of women because these are the stories I have experienced and lived through. These are the stories and characters I can best relay to the community. I not only aim to empower women, but through these stories I share how we can reconnect broken families and communities and protect every spirit's right to live in peace.

Especially since I was at Goddard, I would do a lot of oral history interviews. I found out a lot about my family and their hardships. Most of the time they don't want to talk about the violence, the domestic violence. It was important to tell the stories of the women in my family. I had to tell our stories about the verbal abuse and physical abuse we experienced. I witnessed it. I felt it was important to tell our stories. I wanted to remind them that we couldn't be a community without these strong women. As I was unearthing Hmong and women mythology, I just kept creating performance pieces about Hmong women during the Vietnam War and Secret Wars in Laos. What happened to women during the Vietnam War? How did these women survive the war? I also wrote poetry and stories about my families' experiences. I created a piece to honor my sister who passed away during the war. Another piece was about my father who was a guerrilla soldier during the war. This was a piece I performed at Goddard during my final presentation. I've used these stories in community events. As a whole, I am telling the stories of all the women in my family, and their sacrifices for all of us.

As a youth, I was taught to do service in the community. My grandparents and parents instilled into me a responsibility to community. Later my altruism turned into arrogance because I thought I was saving the world. I started to make assumptions about my fellow community members, such as they were too ignorant or weak to fight for themselves. This wasn't the case at all. In fact, these community members were more resilient and stronger than I was. I have learned from my elders that social change begins when individuals believe in their right to live with dignity.

RUTH: Give an example of resilience.

KAO: In terms of the arts, my parents used their arts to fund important things in their lives. My parents recorded music and sold it in the community to raise money for the church. My mother also used to quilt to earn extra income for the family. I began to see for myself that we weren't ignorant and that we did contribute to this country. I saw the entrepreneurship of my elders and how their arts sustained us physically and spiritually. I learned about internalized oppression. I realized the negative ideas about the Hmong were taught to me from the outside world and my colonizers. In actuality, my elders were so strong; no matter what, they always found a way to keep the family together.

RUTH: What was the turning point for you?

KAO: After college. I started to go into advocacy in Philadelphia when I was sixteen years old. I organized around police brutality and violence against youth. I worked with the Southeast Asian, Latino, and West African communities, helping them gain access to resources. At the time, I still felt that I was educated and better than a lot of folks. It was my responsibility to help these folks get access to resources. It didn't dawn on me that it wasn't a lack of anything, it was a systematic oppression of these communities. It dawned on me because the advocates began to burn out and funds began running out. All of that change was eye-opening to me because then I realized the deeper institutional problems in society. I realized that I didn't have the power to save my community. I thought I could do it on my own but it was impossible.

RUTH: Can you give us an example of this in your work?

KAO: In 2010, I co-choreographed a performance with the spoken-word poet Michelle Myers (of Yellow Rage) in memory of Fong Lee. Fong was a young Hmong youth who was accused of being a gang member and was shot to death by the Minnesota police. Fong Lee's family had been fighting the legal system for several years to bring Fong's unjust murder to the public conscience. I felt it was my duty to raise awareness and funds for Fong and his family through performance. I wanted to support the Lee family and other community activists around the country working to ensure that Jason Andersen, a Minnesota police officer, serve time for unjustly shooting Fong. I felt so disheartened when the legal system exonerated Fong's murderer and the Supreme Court refused to hear the case. I knew the family was devastated because I had been in contact with Fong's sister, Shoua.

Later in the summer of 2011, I had the opportunity of meeting the Lee family in person and to perform for Fong at the site of his murder. It was an emotional performance for me, but I wanted the Lee family, Fong, and my fellow Hmong community members to know that I was fighting with them. My performance would ensure that I had not forgotten Fong. Michelle Myers has connections to poets and artists in Minnesota who had already been working on the case. There were several appeals to get the Supreme Court to review the case. Michelle Myers asked me to co-choreograph a performance piece. She had already written a spoken-word part, so I added traditional Hmong song and dance to the piece. It was a very important statement as a Hmong person. It was happening in our communities all the time: being labeled gang members and violence against our community members, especially our young men. I wanted to make a statement that this was not who the Hmong are or who Fong Lee was. I also wanted to send him to the spirit world with song and dance. He had a troubled youth, but he wasn't a gang member.

There continue to be several cases of shooting of Hmong youth in the Twin Cities and around the country. However, the violence against the young is not exclusively in the Hmong community. Communities around the country continue to witness the murder of their children, such as Trayvon Martin. In Philadelphia, I was always advocating for [justice] and for the end to violence against our youth, especially our Southeast Asian youth.

RUTH: All of the artists we are interviewing use words and something else; for example, words and music or words and movement. What is your lived experience in creating language and having that language brought to life by the use of another art form?

KAO: My Hmong heritage, rich in oral folk arts traditions, has taught me the transference of language is meant to be dynamic. For example, Hmong traditional storytellers use gestures, theater, and song to engage with their audience members. When I began creating my performance pieces, I experimented with many different art forms. I have combined dance, spoken word, and singing in my performance pieces. I have also integrated different languages (Hmong and English) and folk traditions into my performances (Hmong folk songs and dance, African American spirituals, Korean folk dance, and Indian classical dance).

RUTH: Kao, your work speaks to the experience of the Hmong people over many decades. Tell us how you bring your cultural and family background into your work.

KAO: Although I mostly perform in English, the stories I tell and the way in which I convey my stories are from my Hmong heritage. Hmong storytelling is a natural part of me because I have a strong connection to Hmong spirituality. The Hmong are traditionally animists and worshipped their ancestors. My paternal grandfather and my aunt were shamans. My paternal grandmother as well as my maternal grandparents were folksingers and storytellers. These elders greatly influenced my art form.

RUTH: Animist, that is a word that is rarely used. Explain what this term means to the Hmong people. Give us an example of how your elders influence your art.

KAO: Animists are very close to nature and believe that everything around us has a spirit. Everything in the world is connected to each other. If you do something to a rock or a person, there are going to be consequences. That idea, that everything has a life and we are all part of the circle of life is deeply ingrained in me. My parents are now Christians because they were sponsored by Lutherans [when they immigrated to the United States]. However, before my grandparents passed, they were still practicing animism. My grandfather would perform ceremonies when people were sick, and he would perform some of these ceremonies in our house. When my grandparents passed, we held a traditional Hmong funeral.

In the stories that I tell, I think it is because of my spirituality that makes my art Hmong. My intention is not to tell a Hmong story, but my spiritual beliefs do come through in my work. I believe my stories and poetry connect me to everything else—to my ancestors, to other living creatures, and to the Earth. This is what makes it Hmong.

RUTH: You often perform for people who are unfamiliar with Hmong culture. How do you translate this very specific and personal work so that you reach/entertain your audience?

KAO: In many of my past performances, I didn't give much background or even explain the context for my storytelling. I have been told that I should provide more context for the audience so they can better understand my stories. However, I want the community members to interpret for themselves the meanings and lessons of my stories. War, betrayal, anguish, hope, revival, and love are not just a Hmong experience, but human experience. I believe many different community members can make the connections to my stories of struggle and survival.

RUTH: Tell us something I haven't asked but that might interest our readers.

KAO: I have been very interested in Hmong textile lately and hope to incorporate more of this art form into my writing and performance. I am excited to see how this art form will add different layers and texture to my storytelling.

RUTH: Textile and writing and performing. Tell us more.

KAO: When I was performing, I used Hmong flower cloths and textiles for the background, and I have even used cloth in my dance. I want to use Hmong textile in the forefront of my work, though. The storytelling with textile is rich and deep. The Hmong originated in China and have shared a long history with the tribes and peoples emerging from that part of the world. My elders have told me that the Hmong used to have a written language when we lived in China long ago. As the Han Chinese and other ethnic groups expanded their kingdoms and conquered Hmong territories, they attempted to dominate us completely. They killed many Hmong men and forced their practices and language upon the Hmong. Many Hmong families and clans migrated into Southeast Asia to escape Chinese persecution. The Hmong women hid the Hmong written language in our embroidery and textiles, but when they reached Southeast Asia they couldn't decode it. A whole language was lost. I thought this was fascinating. I believe Hmong embroidery is more than decoration. It's warding off evil and protecting the home and spirit. I'm still experimenting with that.

RUTH: What is the experiment?

KAO: I want to add texture to the poetry. Sewing in words and different things into the cloth. The whole movement of creating a [textile] piece while telling a story.

RUTH: Is there a textile that is specifically Hmong?

KAO: There is. In the 1970s and 1980s when Hmong were in Thai refugee camps, Hmong women started creating story textiles, or better known as "Hmong Story Cloth" by Western tourists and countries. These story cloths were sold to generate income for the community. Traditional Hmong clothing has particular geometric shapes and patterns. The Hmong language subgroups, such as the White Hmong, Blue/Green Hmong, and Stripe Hmong, have distinct patterns and styles in their clothing. Another distinctive textile is the baby carriers that contain elaborate geometric shapes and pattern. A very important Hmong textile is the "Elders' Clothing." Children have to prepare special funeral clothing for their parents. These are sewn in a particular way. There are specific purposes for the cloth and Hmong embroidery. These purposes are related to Hmong storytelling, history, and spiritual beliefs.

## Taína Asili: Music for the People

RUTH: When you think of transformative language arts, what comes to mind?

TAÍNA: For me, transformative language arts is about using language with the specific intention of creating personal and social change. Language is extremely powerful, having power over the mind, and even a physical power. Vibrations that are sent out with our speech and song—and there are physical actions in our ears and brain when we receive language. I also believe that language has a spiritual power. And it was this spiritual, mental, and physical power of language that I looked at in my TLA work at Goddard College, specifically, the passing on of ancestral transformative language within Puerto Rican culture, beginning with our African and Taíno ancestors, moving into the present day. What surfaced for me in this work was how the power of language can be used to bring about healing.

RUTH: What does healing mean to you?

TAÍNA: Most typically we think of healing as what happens in our body, curing an illness or injury. But I also think about the social and environmental healing that is so desperately needed in our world right now, the inequality and injustice. Healing to me is also about working on that, about social justice work.

RUTH: How has your affinity with words moved you toward your current profession?

TAÍNA: My roots are in music. I came from a musical family. My father was a musician and my mother was a dancer. My sister and I performed almost from the womb. I started writing poetry at the age of fifteen, as a process of finding my voice, and moving through the racism, sexism, homophobia I experienced in my childhood, and looking more deeply at my identity. Poetry became my healing tool, but I hadn't yet connected poetry and singing.

At sixteen I started to sing in a punk band, Antiproduct, eventually writing songs for the group. I would write poems and put them to the music, creating punk-poetry songs. Through these songs I talked about surviving sexual assault, my struggles to love my body, and finding my power as a woman of color. I was blown away. Every time I sang, it was a musical affirmation of my truth, and other people were strongly resonating with the songs, particularly women. I learned that we are not alone in struggle, and we have the power to fight and heal together. That was when I became a transformative language artist, though it would be more than a decade later before I used that term. I sang with Antiproduct from age sixteen to twenty-two, and the band gathered a large following of fans. We toured the nation several times and released several records all over the world. People still contact me and tell me how the music changed the course of their life and their interest in social justice work. But punk wasn't my musical voice. I left the group because I wasn't fully expressing who I was as a musician. A few years later I reclaimed myself as a TLA artist in other ways.

RUTH: Did you move to another band?

TAÍNA: During my punk years I moved from Binghamton, New York, to Philadelphia, a hub of spoken word, with profound poets like Sonia Sanchez, Lamont B. Steptoe, Amiri Baraka, Ursula Rucker, Jill Scott, and so many others less known. And so I left music for a little while to focus on my poetic self. I did performance poetry for a few years and made a chapbook. That body of work focused primarily on ancestral identity and colonialism. I also became heavily involved in political prisoner justice work, particularly focusing on the case of Mumia Abu-Jamal. This activism deeply informed my artistic work. Political prisoner activism also led me to look at the problem of mass incarceration, which I continue to work on to this day with the New York State Prisoner Justice Network.

In 2004, I received a grant from the Leeway Foundations [funds women and trans artists creating social change] to travel to Puerto Rico to work on some research for a book I was writing. It was going to be a collection of poetry, essays, recipes, and interviews looking at how colonialism has affected our mental, physical, and spiritual health. After this journey, I found Goddard and discovered the TLA program, and I was excited to finish my book as part of my [graduate] work. But what I found was that music is at the core of my artistic expression, and I needed to follow it. So I turned the poetry from my book into lyrics and music and completed my debut album *War Cry* with my new musical project, Taína Asili y la Banda Rebelde. During that time I also received the Transformation Award from the Leeway Foundation, which helped to fund the release of my album.

At Goddard I also developed a poetry workshop curriculum, "Reclaiming Raices," which I have since facilitated with a variety of populations, including incarcerated women, union workers, refugees, and students of all ages. Recently, I have retired this workshop and am now facilitating a new workshop called "Reclaim the Thunder: Songwriting for Social Change."

This year I will be celebrating twenty years as a songwriter for social change, and I am proud of how far I have come, and excited about where I am going. My professional life, as of late, has been a delicate balance of parenting my ten year old and my two year old, holding space for my artistic self, and carving time to do booking and promotion work. Being a transformative language artist means that all of these pieces inform each other, which helps me to keep them balanced. My parenting informs my artistic work, and my social justice work informs the booking and promotion choices I make.

RUTH: What would you say about the power of words to someone who wants to enter your profession?

TAÍNA: As a songwriter/performer, my biggest obstacle has been to accept that my truth is enough and that my story has value and is important. So many of us—particularly people who have been most marginalized in this country and this world—we don't see our truth as having value. It stops us from giving fully what we have to offer this world. It is something that I continue to have to tell myself. I have to write every time before someone interviews me or before I write a song something like "Your story has value." The lesson I continue to learn is that not only does my truth have value but it has power, the power to change the world.

RUTH: What kinds/areas of social change do you aim your work toward?

TAÍNA: I was recently talking with a friend about restorative justice and transformative justice, regarding the prison system. Mass incarceration is a huge problem, but the bigger challenge is to determine how we could deal with these problems in a different way. Restorative justice is fixing what we already have. We have the prison and criminal justice systems, and we are going to do strategic changes within the system to make it better. Transformative justice suggests that rather than changing the system that currently exists, we need to acknowledge that this problem is deeply connected to other injustices that are happening in this world. We need to rethink this whole system. Holding both is important. Social change looks like our personal work that we do within ourselves. That writing I'm doing in my journal is social change work. Social change work looks like service work. It looks like digging deep into our society to look at inequalities and undermine what is happening. There are so many different levels that social change exists on, many of them are really important and have value.

One thing I find really important that I learned from my elders is that it's not how much we do but being consistent with what we do. Don't worry about taking on everything but finding that thing we can offer. I do all kinds of activist work. As I understand myself as an artist, I use my art to dedicate my work. I work with so many types of communities. For example, I went to the SOA protest. They want to shut down the School of the Americas. I performed in the Pacific Northwest and did a workshop at an animal liberation environmental justice conference there. Reclaiming the Thunder: Songwriting for Social Change workshops allow people to dig into what social justice means to them. We use songwriting as a way to express that. My music is only about sharing my own story, my own truth. I offer it as a touchstone for others.

My singing voice needs to carry my words. There is a message; there is a vibration. My words touch people more deeply to the song. I write music that people dance to. Maybe they are not hearing the words right away. I'll talk about the song at some point. The music opens people up to receiving the words better than if I spoke the words. I have found that people are much more open, because of the music, to what I have to say. Music is a vibration. Words carry vibration, singing of the words carries an even greater vibration. I'm also a performer. I bring in the theatrical element to my performance. I've always had a passion for theater. I'm using my full self, using my whole self.

RUTH: What does that look like?

TAÍNA: When I was in the punk scene, it was about how badass you were. It was a performance. I took that power and brought it to spoken word: hand gestures, facial expressions, dance moves. I really try with all my heart to perform my words, perform my music. As I begin a song I close my eyes and try to bring myself within, to the intention of that song. The performance of that song is trying to embody that with my whole self.

RUTH: Taína, your name is related to the Taíno, the people you come from. Tell us how you bring your cultural and family background into your work.

TAÍNA: I'm Puerto Rican and my parents named me Taína so that I would always remember where I came from. My sister's name is Ayana, Swahili for flower. We were given our names so we would remember our African and Taíno indigenous roots. My parents were keepers of culture, folklorists. They played bomba and plena—and they are often joined together—that involved dancing and singing and percussive elements, including drumming. Bomba was used during the time of slavery to practice traditional spiritual ways and honor our humanity and spirit in the face of inhumanity. It was practiced when slave masters went to church, to organize slave revolts. My parents felt it was important to pass these on to my sister and me. They founded a Latin America student union at SUNY-Binghamton. They founded a Latin American cultural organization. They were very involved in being keepers of culture. In my adulthood I claimed this as my own as well. Naming me Taína made sure I never forgot that culture.

In my writing and all the work I do now, this is a continuation of the work they did. The work I do—from the Puerto Rican Independence Movement to work in the holistic health movement—all of that is a continuation of the work to hold onto culture and tradition. Even a fusion or addition to culture is not stagnant. It is ever flowing.

RUTH: You often perform for people who don't have the same background and who may be unfamiliar with the Taíno. How do you translate this very specific and personal work so that you reach/entertain your audience?

TAÍNA: This is where music comes in. Music says things that words can't say. Sometimes I sing in Spanish, and there are English-speakers who don't understand Spanish. Music speaks in a way that words can't. It's important for people to take some time to understand. My story isn't for everybody. My story isn't universal. My work touches whom it touches, and it's not my responsibility to connect with everyone.

## Katt Lissard: Theater For Change

RUTH: When you think of transformative language arts, what comes to mind?

KATT: The first thing that comes to mind is the [MA in Individualized Studies] program at Goddard and the TLA concentration created by Caryn Mirriam-Goldberg. I was originally hired at the college to help "cover" the concentration, but prior to that (I started teaching at Goddard in January

2002), I don't know whether I would have linked those three words together as a rubric for certain kinds/forms of art. I think all the arts have inherent transformative potential, those with and those without verbal, written, spoken, or sung language. Theater, where much of my experience has been, is a combination of verbal, body, visual, and musical language—and I've always seen theater as potentially transformative in a variety of ways for both the audience and the performers.

RUTH: How has your affinity with words moved you toward your current profession?

KATT: Maybe because it's the holiday season, the first thing that comes to mind is when I was a kid we had a really old (ancient, it seemed) three-record set of Charles Dickens' *A Christmas Carol*, which had been my grandmother's. The records were 78s, very heavy and fragile and full of scratches, made out of whatever it was that predated vinyl. The cast was British (with the amazing Ronald Coleman as Scrooge), and it was, essentially, the entire *Christmas Carol*—the story of Ebenezer Scrooge's "transformation" (if you will) via a whole lot of words. By the time I was five years old I knew the entire six sides of the record set by heart (I still know large chunks of it), including the scratchy pauses and those moments where it sounded like the record "swallowed." The story (record 1, side 1) opened with some children singing "God Rest Ye, Merry Gentlemen" and then Scrooge yelling at them: "Get away! Get away, I tell you! I want none of your singing here! Now, get away!" . . . (*scratch, scratch, swallow*). I think for anyone who becomes a writer or an enthusiastic, passionate reader or a theater person (though maybe I'm just speaking for myself), there's probably a pivotal story or tale at a fairly young age, an experience with language, with words, and an experience of being "transported" by language that set things in motion.

RUTH: What struck you about this recording so much that it sticks in your mind today?

KATT: My family was full of storytellers. My maternal grandmother, a New Orleanian who'd been an elocution contest champ at an early age, told us an endless series of what she called "coo-coo stories," each of which centered on an ill-treated person or animal or thing considered inferior or crazy or damaged (i.e., coo-coo) by everyone else, who triumphs or is at least happy in the end. Very predictable, but we loved those stories and always got to pick the protagonist—the mangy stray dog no one wanted or the abandoned bicycle with the broken wheel or the little girl with the limp. My father, on the other hand, was always telling us backwoods Mississippi tall tales full of wordplay in a deep, Southern baritone. I guess I was pulled into the theatricality of the *Christmas Carol* recording. It was exotic. The story was so textured and layered because of the sound effects and the singing and by what the actors were able to do with their voices. There's something about the endurance of particular kinds of tales. I think those highly "moral" tales like *Christmas Carol* we were exposed to as children tend to stick with us (for better or worse) and influence who we are and what we do.

RUTH: Tell us something about the work you do in the theater in Lesotho and at Goddard.

KATT: In Lesotho, through the Winter/Summer Institute, I create collaborative theater with colleagues, students, and villagers about the HIV/AIDS pandemic in the sub-Saharan. We use poetry, music, dance, and a variety of theater-making practices that, essentially, facilitate finding creative ways to express (in live performance) the complicated contexts for the way HIV exists and moves in the culture and society. It's serious work, but we want it to be entertaining and thought-provoking and funny. At Goddard, I work with students in all the concentrations, like TLA, as well as students who are what we call "individualized." My experience has been that people who come into TLA are often looking to combine self-reflection and examining their own history with finding a way to interact with a community and make something in the world that has an impact. I had a student recently who was interested in creating a series of writing workshops for veterans dealing with post-traumatic stress disorder (PTSD). Through the research she did into PTSD and her in-the-field practicum experience, she also ended up dealing with what she recognized as PTSD in her own life—which had a profound effect on her and on what she was doing. People come into TLA wanting to make positive change in the world and find they're transforming themselves in the process.

RUTH: Do you think you've changed by doing some of the work in Lesotho?

KATT: I hope so! For one thing, I'm more aware of how complicated it is for humans to communicate with each other. I have a deeper respect for the nuance of language, whatever that means, whether spoken or nonverbal; and maybe I'm letting go of more assumptions because I understand that I actually have a bunch of assumptions I didn't recognize (or admit) I had before.

RUTH: You are a playwright, an essayist, a teacher, an actor. Much of the work you do involves working with words. If you were mentoring a fledgling playwright—or essayist—what might you say to that person about the power of words?

KATT: I think the most important thing for writers to do is to read, read, read—to find those writers, playwrights, poets that have some impact on them and mean something and to take whatever that experience is and to examine that work closely, to see what works and why/how. An important piece for another recent Goddard student of mine was Rilke's "Letters to a Young Poet." It gave him permission to be out there with his own language, his own experimentation. To explore what was organically there for him. One of the things Rilke says (I'm paraphrasing), if you don't actually have to write, then why are you doing it? You have to feel that you can't live without it. That's the necessity of creating. If it doesn't feel necessary then you're not going to do it. But, you have to read, see, hear, and pursue the things that move you the most. Let yourself be influenced in that sense.

RUTH: What kinds/areas of social change do you aim your work toward?

KATT: The work I've done that most clearly fits into the TLA framework of art and social change is probably the Winter/Summer Institute (WSI). WSI's work began as a response to the devastating HIV/AIDS pandemic in one very small country in Africa (Lesotho) and the idea that theater, created collaboratively, might have some kind of impact, but we haven't had and don't have a "prescriptive" approach to what might constitute change or what, specifically, to change. Our main effort has been to encourage dialogue and to collaborate with communities to discover what might be areas of concern or interest to the community that would be "served" in some way by creating theater *with* us about those areas of concern or interest. There are complex social issues surrounding the HIV pandemic, and over the years some of those complex issues have found theatrical expression through our collaborative work: the impact of gossip and silence on the pandemic, the role that multiple concurrent partnerships (an accepted relational construct in the culture) play in the spread of the virus, the suffocating power of secrets . . .

RUTH: I would think that words—such as gossip—would be extremely powerful in the discourse around HIV/AIDS. Even the phrase "HIV/AIDS" leads to tensions between people and to fear. Can you tell our readers how WSI has opened up or shifted the dialogue about HIV/AIDS?

KATT: We don't just go into a community and present a piece of theater. Like I said, we make theater together, with the community, so we create a platform and a dialogue and a show that comes from the community that's reflective of what the community wants to perform. What is performed, what is seen, is reflective of what actual members of those communities have collaborated with us to create—the work is from the community itself and includes actors from the community. Always and forever we are surprised by what comes out and the issues that come forward. If you don't live some place, how could you really know? I hope we've been part of opening a window, just a bit, where there is some air, some more free-flowing dialogue about certain things. The first year we did this work (2006), talking about condoms in Lesotho was kind of a huge thing and now it's accepted and not a big deal, but that's not just about us, the times and people have changed.

We've also begun to build a theatrical vocabulary, and we know a little more about each other—the villagers from the rural mountain areas and the students from New York, the United Kingdom, South Africa, and Lesotho's National University. Because this is theater, things can be said "creatively" that might not be said otherwise, both in rehearsal and in performance: Words can be put into the mouths of characters and those characters can say to a neighbor or a husband what you can't say yourself, like challenging domestic violence or negotiating to use condoms.

The very first year, as I think I mentioned, our show was based, thematically (we usually have a thematic starting point), on gossip and silence and what a huge obstacle gossip is to getting tested for HIV. Another year the idea people wanted to explore was "secrets make us sick," which played out on a surprising number of levels and included some fairly radical scenes dealing with homosexuality and gender. We spent one year exploring the connection between multiple concurrent partnerships and the spread of the virus.

RUTH: Explain the multiple concurrent partnerships [MCPs].

KATT: Say you and I are married and we each have someone else on the side—someone else we're both aware of because those are also steady long-term outside relationships. And maybe each of our someones on the side has someone, and those people also have someone. No one is being particularly promiscuous. All of those relationships represent a fairly stable and committed network, a multiple concurrent partnership—all of that is fine until the moment something happens (like a breakup) and someone has sex with someone outside the MCP who's infected with HIV. In the first few weeks of transmission the virus is incredibly potent and can infect people quickly, so the entire network, the whole MCP, is suddenly at risk. This is one of the ways the virus is transmitted in the sub-Saharan. We, in WSI, first learned about MCPs from Helen Epstein's book *The Invisible Cure*. She lives in New York and agreed to videotape a talk for us to use in Lesotho. Her talk segued somewhat magically into a presentation for WSI on MCPs by a medical doctor in Lesotho, Dr. Molotsi Monyamane, a co-founder of People Living with AIDS in Lesotho, who started out by joking, "You know how it is—we tell our lover: 'You don't want to use a condom? Come on, it's just you and me . . . and my wife and your boyfriend!'" Which became the title for our show that year (2008)—*It's Just You and Me . . . and My Wife and Your Boyfriend*. It was a dark but often funny show, and in the talk-backs with the audience after those performances there were always a few people who wanted to talk publicly, in the community, about what a revelation it was to them, to realize that these networks they were part of or that they knew others were part of, were putting them all at risk.

RUTH: What it seems you are saying is that just being able to talk about HIV/AIDS can be seen as social change/activism in Lesotho. Why is that?

KATT: Not just in Lesotho—anywhere. We've had students from New York, from the United Kingdom, from Johannesburg, who went home and got tested. Here they were, doing this work, you know, they'd been in this performance talking about this issue and yet they themselves hadn't been tested. It's tricky when your own hypocrisy becomes so evident, you feel compelled to do something about it. That's not a huge "policy" thing but it's significant one-by-one-by-one.

I think we've been part of creating dialogue in communities, but only as a result of collaboration, and not just about HIV, about pretty much everything—poverty, global warming, gender inequity. There are almost always scenes that come up about rape (another avenue of HIV transmission, but much more than that). There was a moment in a particular rape scene we did where the woman goes to the police to report the rape and they laugh at her. This idea of laughing at the victim always came up in the talk-back after the show. I remember one man in the audience who was so infuriated and ashamed by that laughter he could barely speak, but he felt he *had* to. So it became a public dialogue: Why do we do that, as humans, laugh at victims instead of taking action, instead of stepping in?

RUTH: Katt, your work involves co-creating productions with community members. Tell us something about your approach to collaborating with communities—especially communities you're not a part of. You might talk about your work in Lesotho or in other areas of the world with cultural expectations, artistic expressions or aesthetics that differ from your own. How do you incorporate your cultural background into the work you do?

KATT: We use a lot of humor and a lot of music, and we consciously avoid "handing down the word" or "giving out a message"—as we say in the description of WSI: "We strive to be the opposite of 'message' theater, building our performance through an improvisational process that weeds out anything that doesn't make us laugh or pull us in or cause us to think."

In our most recent international iteration of WSI, we were brainstorming with villagers in the Malealea Valley, a rural area up in the mountains of Lesotho where we've worked since WSI began. We were in what we call the "gathering" phase of our work. The gathering phase takes place after we arrive in the rural areas and have performed for the nearby communities in front of the area's health clinic or school. This initial performance has been created by our university student participants in collaboration with faculty facilitators and is the very first thing we do when we get to Lesotho: Students and faculty from the three or four universities spend an intense few weeks together creating a show that comes from the students' issues and concerns, which we then use as the springboard to create more work in collaboration with rural villagers.

We were in the "gathering phase" after the performance of that springboard show—and we were in small groups with village participants asking what had worked for them, what might have rung true, and, more importantly, what might be missing that they wanted to create. In other words, what do we keep, what do we throw away, and what do we need to make together that comes from "here" (i.e., from the village)? We "gather" these reactions, thoughts, creative ideas, phrases, and then we move on from there to make new scenes with the villagers.

There are always many responses and reactions and ideas—and there are always a lot of things that come up that are surprising and exciting because there are things we'd never know or hear about or be given "access" to if we didn't come into a kind of community with people by first sharing something with them and then asking: *What did we get right? What did we get wrong? What should be here that isn't?* It's important to note that it's not just the foreigners who wouldn't be privy to all of this, it's also the National University of Lesotho students who, even if they came from a rural area originally, are seen as very "other" by villagers once they've entered the university because they're now of a different social class.

We're always provocatively surprised and often chastened by the gravity of what comes up during these initial collaborative sessions. In this particular session one of the villagers whispered, "Girls are disappearing from the villages and no one is talking about it!"

That hushed exclamation touched on so many different (and complicated) issues all at the same time: sex trafficking, poverty, gender inequity, the spread of HIV, the social hierarchy (even in bare-bones villages) of those girls who might be targeted and those not, the fact that "*no one is talking about it!*" for multiple reasons. In the show we created with that community, the line is whispered in both English and Sesotho (the official language of Lesotho) over and over again—*Girls are disappearing from the villages and no one is talking about it!*—as the transition out of one scene and into another, where a village girl is lured away by a slick procurer with the promise of "a job in town." The job proposition includes a nice wad of cash given by the procurer to the girl's family, which he presents as a loan the girl could repay once her fabulous job begins. The more we worked on the scene with the village actors, the more obvious it became that the specifics of what we were creating were drawn from a participant's recent, shattering experiences. Lesotho's villages are often desperately poor and part of the shame of this particular secret, and one of many reasons "no one is talking about it," has to do with poverty and the way people are manipulated because of it. We might all say we understand poverty is a universal ingredient in sex trafficking—maybe *the* universal ingredient—but breaking that down to an individual example, performed live, was really potent.

That's an example of co-creating with community members that was pretty straightforward and went pretty well. A more complicated example would be this: Every time we've worked with a rural community, typically, a storyline comes up or a scene is proposed about taking a person sick with HIV to the *sangoma* (*traditional healer*) and to the health clinic and to the priest or preacher. Also, typically, the clinic usually "wins" the contest of which of these is the "best" treatment for the one who is ill. On a recent trip there was a heated debate between those who were "for" the clinic and those who were "for" the *sangoma* and those who were "for" religion/prayer. On one hand, this was a positive development because we were being brought into the intricacies and nuances of the debate instead of the village performers choosing to take the easy route and just appease what they presumed were our outsiders' expectations—that is, someone sick with HIV should go to the health clinic. On the other hand, the scene that came out of this more nuanced approach was overly fraught and interminable. The upside was that, eventually, we were able to turn it into a scene that took all the conflicting solutions (Western medicine, traditional medicine, religion) and presented them in a highly provocative but satiric way, which left the door open to multiple resolutions depending on the needs of the sick person. In the end, the HIV-positive person was taking ARVs (antiretroviral medications) from the clinic, using herbs prescribed by the *sangoma*, and his mother was praying for him. Which, when you think about it, is exactly what people do everywhere—rarely does someone only go to the doctor or to the alternative healer or to the minister. We all approach illness through multiple routes and seek out multiple paths to a cure.

RUTH: Tell me something about your work I haven't asked but that might interest our readers.

KATT: I continue to experiment with exploring where theatrical expression and my subjective, outsider observations of Africa intersect and what might happen at the juncture where they meet. Right now, in New York, I'm working on a theatre piece called *Surrogate Traveler*, which has a lot to do with the central characters not understanding a language and attempting to understand a culture when they are "other" to both of those things—the language, the culture—and, yet, they are constantly filling in the blanks and contextualizing the world around them, all the while unaware that their own context is the stumbling block, the deaf ear.

## *Snapshot*

### Kelley Hunt, Lawrence, Kansas

*Singer-songwriter, international touring and teaching artist*

The main focus of my life has always been music, with an emphasis on songwriting. I've made my living as a songwriter, performer, and recording artist most of my adult life. Along the way, I've composed for film, television, and nonprofit groups, and put out five critically acclaimed CDs, with a sixth one in the works. My music, as well as how I make a living, is diverse: rhythm and blues, jazz, rock, Americana, blues, roots, and gospel. I'm mostly giving back to both my local and national communities by donating either performances or use of some of my songs to generate funds for charities.

After decades of touring with the Kelley Hunt Band and on my own, in the last ten or so years I've been compelled to branch out and facilitate workshops on singing, songwriting, blues/gospel piano, performance skills in both traditional school settings (K–12, college) and nontraditional, including "Brave Voice: Writing & Singing for Your Life," a six-day retreat along with Caryn Mirriam-Goldberg. I've collaborated with other artists most of my life, whether it's through writing songs, performing, scoring films, or putting together performances that bring in dance, poetry, and other arts.

I love that I have something uniquely my own to "give," specifically, a way to lift people's spirits, inspire them to do their own creative work, feel the camaraderie and healing aspects of group singing, and generally feel better.

www.kelleyhunt.com

# Snapshot

## Deb Hensley, Freedom, Maine

*Singer-songwriter, writer, consultant, facilitator, and TLA Network coordinator*

I help people explore a variety of vocal exploration possibilities through workshops, consulting, and writing and performing original songs; yet the most relevant daily work I'm currently doing around TLA is serving as the coordinator for the TLA Network. Through this work I am supported in my own creative efforts, but I also have the privilege of opening my heart much wider in support of the TLA work of others. It is a joy to refer these fine artists to one another, to help them promote their artistic work toward personal and social change, and to offer them the resources and connections to do so. This is such a dynamic network—remarkably free of "ego," because the focus is so clearly on the *transformative power* of the written, spoken, and sung word rather than status or personal gain.

My own TLA work in recent years blends music, writing, and community into a tapestry of change. Probably the most satisfying and innovative work has been co-founding Maine's premier five-member vocal improvisation a cappella ensemble, Improvox, which performed regionally and nationally as well as at leading vocal exploration workshops that build a sense of community through the sung word. This group has spawned literally hundreds of vibrant singing circles around the Northeast and has recently shifted to a "singing collective" model, coming together in new ways to do this collaborative work. I'm thrilled to be performing original and improvisational music with a new trio called Flash Tonic, presenting school residencies with same; introducing vocal improvisation forms and games to elementary school children, including the spoken word.

I regularly bring the sung word, through vocal improvisation, into the early childhood education consulting work that I've done around the country for the past decade. I take particular delight in helping teachers, educators, and parents reinhabit their voices and discover new educational ideas through the "word of song" in my workshops and trainings. Nothing introduces a concept or solidifies meaning better than a good improvised call-and-response singing session and resulting circle song!

Leading workshops and sharing my story modeled on my Goddard graduate presentation "I Shall Go Singing" comes out of a year of listening to birdsong and composing songs based on this deep listening that has resonated with many—much more than I'd ever have imagined. This project—a presentation and a collection of songs I've composed to interpret a variety of bird songs in my backyard—brings together ecological arts, deep listening, music composition, performing, visual arts, and spiritual practice.

Songwriting continues to draw me like a tide lifting me above despair and discouragement toward my truest identity. I play out locally in duo with another female singer-songwriter. Through interactive singing performances we explore and celebrate our personal stories and transformations as women, and share with other people—women especially—the freedom singing and songwriting can bring out personally and communally.

Toni Morrison speaks of the "blue door" through which we walk to dwell in the creative place. I light up when I walk through the blue door, whether to write songs, fiction, poetry, or to sing and perform. Through the sung word, I want to invite others to walk through that blue door with me to shift their inner landscape.

www.whendidwestopsinging.com

7

# Theopoetics as a Spiritual Form of Transformative Language Arts

CALLID KEEFE-PERRY

> How does Truth prosper among you?
>
> —*Traditional Quaker Query*

In 1991, poet, critic, and one-time National Endowment for the Arts chairperson Dana Gioia published a book that contained one of the most important literary essays of the last century. *Can Poetry Matter?* takes its title from an article Gioia wrote that was first printed in *The Atlantic Monthly* of May 1991, garnering hundreds of letters of response, and inciting a firestorm of discussion. At its core was a plain-spoken articulation of the decline of readership and relevance for American poetry:

> Decades of public and private funding have created a large professional class for the production and reception of new poetry comprising legions of teachers, graduate students, editors, publishers, and administrators. Based mostly in universities, these groups have gradually become the primary audience for contemporary verse. Consequently, the energy of American poetry, which was once directed outward, is now increasingly focused inward. (Gioia, 1991)

As goes poetry, so goes theology, which often has turned too far into disciplinary self-reflection, becoming an echo chamber of jargon, disconnected from the voices of the people in communities for whom theologians truly do have care and commitment. In spite of this, there is much to suggest that something else is on the horizon.

In the past decade, academic interest in the field of theology has seen the slight rise and recovery of a concept first articulated in the early 1970s. This idea, termed *theopoetics*, has its roots in biblical and literary studies and an awareness of language's slipperiness. Rather than affirming imperial, dominant "must be true" theologies, theopoetics gestures toward the importance of affirming communal interpretation and the value of the particular and local. While this perspective is certainly not only found in theopoetics—womanist, liberation, and queer theologies are clear on this point as well—there is a more marked emphasis on the creative and aesthetic in theopoetics. Via a theopoetic lens, Truth with a capital "T" is something that lives and grows: it is vital, verdant, and expanding, not fixed or complete. It isn't a denial that "the truth" might be an actual thing, but a reminder that even assuming that is the case, we humans are creatures of endless interpretation and context. We tell stories in our communities that carry forward memories of power and truth, and these stories become our lenses, inspire our actions, and fuel the fires of further story. Theopoetics affirms the importance of this cycle of creation and encourages the formal, technical discipline of academic theology to affirm the importance of this as well.

Here I detail the origins of theopoetics as well as its current state in academia. I then move to highlight parallels between some key texts from both theopoetics and TLA, drawing insights from the work of Amos Wilder, Rubem Alves, James Sparrell, and David Abram. As the former coordinator of the TLA Network, the present chairperson of the Network's Leadership Council, someone who serves in the ministry within the Religious Society of Friends (Quakers), and the author of *Way to Water: A Theopoetics Primer*, I'm conveniently situated to see the ways in which these two fields are resonant. From theopoetics I think those interested in TLA can find a model for undergirding work in engaged spirituality, and from TLA I think those interested in theopoetics will find inspiration for engaging in empowering, creative work in communities.

## Origins

It is at the level of the imagination that the fateful issues of our new world-experience must first be mastered. It is here that culture and history are broken, and here that the church is polarized. Old words do not reach across the new gulfs, and it is only in vision and oracle that we can chart the unknown.

—*Amos Wilder (1976, 1)*

Before looking at current work being done in theopoetics and the ways in which that work can be understood as a form of practicing TLA as engaged spirituality, it is worth briefly sharing the beginnings of theopoetics. I will provide an overview intended merely to help contextualize the idea, offering a slight sketch of the history so as to help readers get their bearings.

Although the *term* theopoetics may be unfamiliar, the ideas that surround it are often intuitive for many people. Each of the following is a quality of what is often associated with the early writing on theopoetics:

- Affirmation that religious language is more art and less science.
- A turn towards the particular and the embodied rather than what Bible scholar Amos Wilder called "wan and bloodless abstraction."
- Simultaneous attention to precision of language *and* to knowing language cannot capture everything perfectly.
- A distinct lack of emphasis on positing certain "proof of God," favoring instead work that attempts to evoke recognition and experience.
- An attempt to balance and honor the deep traditions of spiritual practice and interpretation with individual experience of the divine in the present.

Those that identify their work with theopoetics are likely to affirm Wilder's claims that (1) "religious communication generally must overcome a long addiction to the discursive, the rationalistic, and the prosaic," and that (2) "the Christian imagination must go halfway to meet the new dreams, mystiques, and mythologies that are gestating in our time" (Wilder, 1976, 1).

More than twenty years before Wilder's *Theopoetic* (1976) was published, he argued that when considering scripture "we cannot apply . . . our modern alternatives of literal versus symbolic. They were meant neither literally nor symbolically" (Wilder, 1955a, 11). In his 1933 dissertation, he wrote that "on the one hand we take [scriptures] too literally and ignore the poetical mentality of the race and the age. On the other hand we make a mistake if we think of them as merely symbol and poetry as a modern would understand them" (Wilder, 1933, 7). What emerges in Wilder's thought is not an *either/or* kind of thinking, but a robust *both/and* theological reflection on literature's ability to have us see the strange in the familiar and the familiar in the strange. Indeed, Wilder was clear that how we see and experience the world is strongly influenced by the ways we have learned to talk about the world. Language is not merely a tool we employ to describe a concrete reality; rather, words contribute to how it is we understand that reality in the first place.

Any human language represents a special kind of order superimposed upon existence. Generations live in it as a habitat in which they are born and die. Outside it is nescience. The language of a people is its fate. Thus the poets or seers who purify the language of the tribe are truly world-makers and the "unacknowledged legislators of the world." Perhaps one can say that nothing affects the significance of human existence more than the range and resource of our articulation, vocabulary, syntax, and discourse. People awaken to a greater plenitude of being as they operate with more signs and names and media of communication, and so find themselves more aware of their world and its interrelationships (Wilder, 1971, 5–6).

Though Wilder had been exploring these kinds of ideas for nearly forty years, it is not until the late 1960s that—borrowing the word from Stanley Hopper—he began using the term theopoetics to describe the field of thinking. Hopper himself is actually where the term originates; his 1971 lecture "The Literary Imagination and the Doing of Theology" is the first published piece of scholarship to make direct use of the term theopoetic (Hopper, 1967, 3–4). In that talk Hopper optimistically claims that humanity is in a period in which we will begin the "radical revisioning of our way of seeing and thinking" (Hopper, 1992, 207). He suggests that the question at hand for theology is not how to develop new, socially relevant approaches, but something more drastic: He asks "whether theology, insofar as it retains methodological fealty to traditional modes, is any longer viable at all" (207). This question is as relevant today—perhaps more so—as it was then.

Hopper himself had been immersed for years in explorations at the intersection of theology and literature. From 1948 to 1950 Hopper chaired the Commission on Literature at the National Council of Churches and was the only representative from the United States at the First Conference on Religion and the Arts at the Ecumenical Institute of Celigny, Switzerland, in 1958. That same year, at Drew University, he founded the first graduate program in theology and literature in the United States.

Throughout his life he had a profound personal predilection toward the arts, was a published poet himself, and was close friends with both Cleanth Brooks and T. S. Eliot (Miller, 2000, 1–2). Without the work of Hopper and the ways in which Wilder made use of that scholarship, contemporary conversations about theopoetics would be drastically different—if present at all. Their affinities for the poetic encouraged them to proceed with theology that tries to see the strange in the familiar and the familiar in the strange, to question stagnant systems of power, and to empower communities to help self-name their condition.

Having grown from the vision of Hopper and Wilder, theopoetics enacts a kind of theological form of TLA in that it works to develop inspiration and tools that can be passed on to those looking for ways to be transformative and creative leaders in communities of faith. Theopoetics affirms the legitimacy of a community challenging oppressive systems, encouraging them to explore what happens when they reenvision and rename the world in ways that dismantle harmful structures and create more generative and just narratives.

## Theopoetics Today

[theopoetics is] an acceptance of cognitive uncertainty regarding the Divine, an unwillingness to attempt to unduly banish that uncertainty, and an emphasis on action and creative articulation regardless. It also suggests that when the dust has settled after things have been said and done in the name of God, the reflection and interpretation to be done ought to be grounded in dialogue and enacted with a hermeneutic of hospitality and humility, an acceptance of cognitive uncertainty regarding the Divine, an unwillingness to attempt to unduly banish that uncertainty.

—*Callid Keefe-Perry (in press)*

As of 2014, there are twenty or so academics who have published work somehow related to theopoetics. If we consider graduate students writing papers and dissertations, there are perhaps fifty or sixty. As of the year 2000, there were no courses being taught specifically about theopoetics, and now there are at least nine degree-granting institutions that have offered graduate-level classes and seminars on the topic. What's more, with that list of schools including Harvard, Drew, Boston University, and the Claremont School of Theology, there is reason to believe the conversation will continue to receive increasing attention.

There is no certain clarity at this point, but at least one strong theme has surfaced that seems likely to be the catalyst for some significant portion of the theopoetic work of the future. Minister and nonviolent activist trainer Matt Guynn (2010) has perhaps been the most articulate in regard to this emergent theme:

> There is a risk that theopoetics will remain just a conversation corner in the academy. Yes, the writing may evoke more writing, but these rivers of words deserve to also flow into the sanctuary and toward the streets. If theopoetics is to keep growing toward its real promise of more powerful engagements with Mystery-Absence-God-Presence, then theopoetics will need to find life not only in the pages of journals, but also in worship services that midwife the new/ancient humanity, and in incarnate experiments of struggles for justice/peace. (106)

If the full measure of theopoetics is to be realized, it must emerge in communities of *practice* and not just in the minds and papers of the thinkers who have conceived of its value. This is hardly a novel idea. There is a fairly constant refrain among progressive Christian theologians that we must work harder to increase the relevance of our scholarship to folks outside of the academy. Yet in the case of theologians who engage with theopoetics the situation is all the more pointed. If we affirm the importance of individual perspectives and work to encourage an understanding of each voice "as it is woven together with other voices" (May, 1989, 165), to remain in integrity with our claims, I believe we must *actively* work to engender communities of Truth-seeking and Truth-speaking.

Patrick Reyes argues a similar point, framing theopoetics as a "destabilizing, decentering, and decolonizing language" that can serve to help marginalized communities respond to oppression by catalyzing "acts of *poiesis*, the creative act calling forth the new community" (Reyes, in press). For Reyes the promise of theopoetics is that it "provides marginalized communities a language to play out their contemporary struggles using spiritual, biblical and suppressed knowledges" (Reyes, in press). By allowing for an understanding of Truth-seeking and Truth-speaking that affirms the importance of communal interpretation and the community's mastery over its own experience, theopoetics invites the possibility that "suppressed knowledges" will be given voice and assist in the transformation or "waking up" of that community. By encouraging communities to value the inherent spiritual wisdom *already contained* in the lives and bodies of those present, we encourage the dismantling of systems of structural oppression, which insist that outside experts must be consulted when the going gets tough.

Reyes gives an example of local explorations of "divine love" in his home of Alisal, California, citing the work of local poet Adela Castillo (Castillo, 2006; 2009) and the "theopoetic" hip-hop lyrics of local rappers and prophets, *Pocas Palabras*:

> *Pocas Palabras*, few words, offer their theopoetic insight . . . in a song entitled "Dream," inspired by Dr. King's "I Have a Dream" speech . . . [The song] beckons youth in the community to "dream" with the Gods of their reality, the Aztec Gods noted by the word *Tonalli*, representing for these artists the Nahuatl word referencing one's soul or energy source planted in the head of the individual by the Gods before birth. The *Tonalli* connects and drives a person to their destiny. Theopoetics in this hue engenders and calls forward the Gods of the community for the purpose of changing the community, to appeal to the God-given life force of individuals to have the power and courage to change their world. More importantly, *Pocas Palabras* focus on how such a theopoetics energizes the dream where everyone has a voice, where all theopoetics are heard. (Reyes, in press)

As theopoetics moves forward I believe that it will do so in work like Reyes has done, embedded in a place and in love with a people that have words for the world—words that encourage more words and more action: new insight, new liberation, new Truth.

Though not connected in any direct way with the Quakers, the spirit of theopoetics shares much with the Quaker idea of "continuing revelation," the notion that "God's revelation for humanity is unfolding, or that at least the human understanding of God's will may change in changed circumstances, and new experience of Truth may add new dimensions to received faith" (Dandelion, 2011, 86). Put another way, although those who embrace a theopoetic perspective may well have a great respect for the importance and authority of holy texts, they also are aware that how we understand what those texts mean is not fixed. We seek after Truth not as some trophy or prize but as a seed we must nurture so it continues to grow. Centuries before French critical theory and postmodernism, Quakers understood that truth was something that "prospered," not something that was obtained or acquired once and for all. Indeed, one of the earliest prayerful reflections that Quakers issued for regular consideration was the brief question posed in the opening epigraph: How does Truth prosper among you? (Hoffman, 2011, 289).

Theopoetics attempts to support the prospering of Truth in communities, affirming the legitimacy and power of personal perspectives and encouraging communities to look to one another, as well as to external experts, for guidance. Indeed, it is precisely in its emphasis on communal empowerment that theopoetics can best be seen as a form of religious thought resonant with TLA. Each of the five core values that undergird the practice of TLA—cooperation, community-building, empowerment, collective wisdom, and sustainability—are also vital to the theopoetic.

*Cooperation* is essential because the theopoetic is not at home in debate or theological proof; rather, spaces of mutual growth, dialogue, and expression are valued. *Community-building* is an explicit focus of the theopoetic because we hope that the new-words and new-naming of spiritual experience is not merely aesthetics for aesthetics' sake, but for the marking of new—or renewed—communities and ways of seeing and being with one another. *Empowerment* is a necessary component of theopoetics, and the power and legitimacy of *collective wisdom* is named and affirmed. Finally, theopoetics also reflects the value of *sustainability* because it encourages communities to authentically name their conditions, their experience of God—or their experience of God's absence—and to allow their voices to be raised instead of repeating words that may have begun to lose their power and verve. Theopoetics allows communities to grow and change rather than become stagnant.

## Theopoetics as TLA via Engaged Spirituality

In the hundreds of conversations in my role as TLA Network coordinator, I explain transformative language arts as a broad category meant to encompass any who make use of language in an artistic way for positive personal and/or communal change. By casting the net broadly like this we are able to bring together people from a variety of disciplines who might not otherwise meet but who are all seeking after the same vision: the world transformed with words. Poets and pastors, grant-writers, journaling experts, therapists, rappers, and rabbis—each can come around a table marked for those who see the power of the language arts as a source for transformation.

Under that general rubric it would seem that theopoetics fits quite nicely as a TLA version of theology. In fact, some of the writing long associated with the practice of TLA is entirely applicable to theopoetics as well. In his piece "A TLA Ethic as Conscious, Connected, and Creative Action," James Sparrell (2007) writes that ethical practice in a TLA context will likely result in coming into relationship with the community and the local world in new and unexpected ways. Rather than simply imparting (or bestowing) knowledge, TLA practice seeks to pursue understanding and discovery so that both the TLA practitioner and the relevant community will experience change and construct new understanding.

This is precisely the kind of thing that Guynn and Reyes envision as the possibility—and necessary future—of theopoetics. Rather than working out theological concepts with the primary referent being other theological concepts, theopoetics takes its cues from the lives and stories of lived experience, from the metaphors and quandaries of actual people of faith. This doesn't deny the value of theological insight and articulation, but it asks that it be done with an ear to the Earth and with an eye to the particulars of place.

Delighting in the multitudinous ways in which the Divine gives rise to thought and symbol, theopoetics is not merely concerned with paying attention to the particulars of a place. Indeed, liberation theologies are already that: articulations of theological thought emerging from the particulars of a place where people are marginalized and oppressed. Theopoetic thought encourages this *and* wonders aloud if the emerging thought needs to be voiced in a different timbre than what has come before. Rubem Alves, a notable Brazilian contributor to theopoetic literature, draws out this distinction well, noting in an interview that he had begun to become dissatisfied with liberation theology, because "it had little to say about the personal dimension of life. If a father or mother comes with their dead child, it's no consolation to say, 'In the future just society there will be no more deaths of this kind.' This brings no comfort!" (Puleo, 1984, 193). Instead, Alves has an alternative vision for a liberative theology, one which maintains "an erotic exuberance for life" and the "need to struggle to restore its erotic exuberance, to share this with the whole world" (194). This fully fleshed desire to be simultaneously pragmatic about justice *and* to pay attention to the particular is also strongly present in the work of those who identify as practicing TLA. Consider the following two examples drawn from members of the TLA Network (2014):

> A storytelling class for caretakers of people with terminal illnesses meets weekly for two months. The participants, all of whom have lost a loved one to a terminal illness at least six months before, tell stories mostly at first about loss, grief, anger, exhaustion, hopelessness, and depression. As they revise and hone their stories, and witness others who have been through similar circumstances, the participants begin to give themselves permission to create new stories about what they want in their lives now and in the future. They perform their work together at a special event held at a local respite center.

> A writing class for inmates in a maximum security prison allows a group of men a chance to write about "the story behind the story" of their crimes: the family and community conditions that drew them into crime in the first place. In writing about their childhoods, particularly how poverty and often growing up without a father impacted their lives, they develop a deeper understanding about not only why they're in prison, but what other options they may have once their terms are over.

In neither example are easy answers given or all the problems magically resolved. Those who have lost loved ones still feel the ache of an empty bed or home, and the men serving time still can only but hope to wake to more than gray walls. And yet, through naming the details of their losses, longing, and pain, they transform their present reality into one in which the hope of a changed future seems more possible. They honor the importance of the experience of what is, not trying to dash it away with what should be. Not just promises of a just world to come for a crying mother with a lost child, but a measure of comfort and grace, an acknowledgment of the pain and how little sense it makes.

Another strong case of the resonance between these fields comes from David Abram. His biography often names him as a "cultural ecologist, philosopher, and spiritual teacher," and his work explores the ways in which our imagination has been shaped by various cultural narratives, resulting in a diminished relationship with the natural world. He engages easily with resources from Jewish mysticism to Maurice Merleau-Ponty and from indigenous shamans on Bali to the hard biological sciences of ecology. His most significant work to date, *Spell of the Sensuous*, takes as one of its major concerns the question of how "the manner in which the style of our discourse—our way of wielding words—tacitly works to either enable, or to stifle, the solidarity between the human community and the more-than-human earth" (Abram, 2005, 172). Put another way, Abram's work is the same encouragement that Amos Wilder wanted, namely, to help "people awaken to a greater plenitude of being as they operate with more signs and names and media of communication, and so find themselves more aware of their world and its interrelationships" (Wilder, 1971, 6).

Abram is also directly associated with TLA. He has been a keynote presenter at the Network's Power of Words conference and was a contributor to the first TLA anthology. Indeed, his article in that book contains numerous refrains that would be equally at home in the conversations surrounding theopoetics. Consider, for example, the following:

> I'm not saying that we should renounce abstract reason and simply abandon ourselves to our senses, or that we should halt our scientific questioning and the patient, careful analysis of evidence. Not at all: I'm saying that as thinkers and as scientists we should strive to let our insights be informed by our direct, sensory experience of the world around us; and further, that we should strive to express our experimental conclusions in a language accessible to direct experience, and so to gradually bring our science into accord with the animal intelligence of our breathing bodies. . . . Sensory experience, when honored, renews

> the bond between our bodies and the earth. Only a culture that disdains and dismisses the senses could neglect the living land as thoroughly as our culture neglects the land. (Abram, 2007, 117)

Replace "science" with "theology" in the above passage, and Abram's argument is only a hair's breadth away from Alves' call for "an erotic exuberance for life" and Wilder's claim that "the chief obstacle to [faith] is the stultifying axiom that genuine truth or insight or wisdom must be limited to that which can be stated in discursive prose, in denotative language stripped as far as possible of all connotative suggestions, in 'clear ideas,' in short, in statement or description of a scientific character" (Wilder, 1955b, 60). Each calls for a greater acceptance of the value of the experiential and the communal. Each believes that more attention to "our breathing bodies" will bring with it hopes for connection and liberation.

## Conclusion

Given the degree to which the world is in need of healing, celebration, and transformation, the fact that training and work in TLA is an option is a blessing. What I hope I've shown here is that for all of the ways that contemporary theology and religion can be construed as destructive and counterproductive to progress and liberation, there is certainly a way forward that makes room for joy, connection, and justice. So: Can poetry matter? Can *theology* matter? Yes, but to do so, those disciplines—those *arts*—must actively redirect their energy, returning again to face out into communities and the feeling of life being lived.

"Transformative language arts" is the phrase we use to point out that language—used with intention and with an eye to the artistic and the communal—and it can be catalytic for the deepening of relationships and experiences of healing, liberation, and celebration. I hope that if someone asks if TLA is being practiced in the fields of theology and ministry, people will be able to say, "Yes. We call that theopoetics. It helps Truth to prosper."

# References

Abram, David. 2005. Between the body and the breathing earth: A reply to Ted Toadvine. *Environmental Ethics*, 27:171–90.

——. 2007. Waking our senses: Language and the ecology of sensory experience. In *The power of words: Social and personal transformation through the spoken, written, and sung word*, eds. Caryn Mirriam-Goldberg and Janet Tallman, 113–26. Keene, NH: TLA Press.

Castillo, Adela. 2006. Mondo Mio. Editorial. *La quimera*.

——. 2009. *Sólo amor*. Orbi Press.

Dandelion, Ben. 2011. Continuing revelation. In *Historical dictionary of the Friends (Quakers)*, eds. Margery Post Abbott, Mary Ellen Chijioke et al., 86. Plymouth, UK: Scarecrow.

Gioia, Dana. 1991. Can poetry matter? *The Atlantic Monthly*. http://www.theatlantic.com/past/unbound/poetry/gioia/gioia.htm (accessed August 2013).

Guynn, Matthew. 2010. Theopoetics and social change. *Cross Currents*, 60(1):105–14.

Hoffman, Jan. 2011. Queries. In Abbott, Chijioke et al., *Historical dictionary of the Friends (Quakers)*, 289.

Hopper, Stanley. 1992. The literary imagination and the doing of theology. In *The way of transfiguration: Religious imagination as theopoiesis*, eds. R. Melvin Keiser and Tony Stoneburner, 207–29. Louisville, KY: Westminster/John Knox.

——. 1967. Introduction. In *Interpretation: The poetry of meaning*, ed. David L. Miller. New York: Harcourt Brace.

Keefe-Perry, L. Callid. In press. In *Way to water: A theopoetics primer*. Eugene, OR: Cascade.

——. 2009. Theopoetics: Process and perspective. *Christianity and literature*, 58(4):579–601.

May, A. Melanie. 1989. *Bonds of unity: Women, theology and the worldwide church*. Atlanta: Scholars.

Miller, David. 2000. "Stanley Hopper and mythopoetics." Speech delivered February 5 for the 40th anniversary meeting of the society for the arts, religion and contemporary culture. http://www.sarcc.org/Hopper.htm (accessed November 9, 2012).

——, ed. 1967. *Interpretation: The poetry of meaning.* New York: Harcourt Brace.

Puleo, Mev. 1994. Rubem Alves. In *The struggle is one: Voices and visions of liberation*, 185–204. Albany: SUNY Press.

Reyes, Patrick Bruner. In press. Alisal: Theopoetics and emancipatory politics. *THEOPOETICS*, 3(1).

Sparrell, James. 2007. A TLA ethic as conscious, connected, and creative action. In Mirriam-Goldberg and Tallman, *The power of words*, 279–87.

TLA Network. 2014. TLA in action. http://www.tlanetwork.org/about/tla-in-action/ (accessed February 12, 2014).

Wilder, Amos N. 1976. *Theopoetic: Theology and the religious imagination.* Philadelphia: Fortress.

——. 1971. *Early Christian rhetoric.* Cambridge, MA: Harvard University Press.

——. 1955a. Scholars, theologians, and ancient rhetoric. *Journal of Biblical Literature*, 75:1–11.

——. 1955b. *New Testament faith for today.* New York: Harper.

——. 1933. The relation of eschatology to ethics in the teaching of Jesus as represented in Matthew. PhD diss., Yale University.

# Snapshot

## Larry Greer, Alfred, Maine

*Interfaith minister and pastoral coordinator*

In my work as an Interfaith minister and pastoral coordinator for Hospice of Southern Maine for the past ten years, I use poetry and metaphor as part of a holistic approach to good spiritual care at end of life. Poetry serves as a catalyst that brings forth the deeper inner self and allows a freedom of expression within a safe (dare I say sacred?) space.

Since I've become a pastoral coordinator, I have provided many educational opportunities for the community at large, including a five-week series entitled "Facing Death and Finding Spiritual Hope," in which participants are led through a series of journaling, art, poetry and other exercises to create a deeper awareness of our own mortality. I also organize, through Hospice of Southern Maine, the annual Thresholds conference, which features music, art, and dance, as well as national and international speakers, such as the Reverend Dr. Kathleen Rusnak, author of *Because You Have Never Died Before*; Maggie Callanan, co-author of *Final Gifts* and author of *Final Journeys*; Dr. Ira Byock, author of *Getting the Best Care Possible* and the poet laureate of Portland, Maine.

Sharing poetry from the mystical voice is a way to enter the world of the dying with gentleness and purpose. From the moment of diagnosis, one's world is turned upside down with the questions of a lifetime, particularly the unknown. I have been blessed many times when I've helped hospice patients and those who work with them read and write poetry. Hearing their words read back to them in a loving, nonjudgmental voice validates feelings, fears, hopes, and love.

## *Snapshot*

### Joanna Tebbs Young, Rutland, Vermont

*Writer, columnist, expressive writing and spirituality workshop facilitator, and workshop developer*

It was almost exactly ten years ago when I woke up one morning with the realization that I wanted to teach others how to journal. I designed a workshop based on Marlene Schiwy's *A Voice of Her Own*, and while researching I discovered Kathleen Adams' Center for Journal Therapy (CJT).

I was eventually certified as a Journal to the Self instructor through CJT, and I have been running workshops, coaching clients, and guest speaking since 2009. I am a columnist for two local papers, freelance copywriter, and a blogger.

I facilitate my workshops around the community or in my writing center, The Writers' Room at Allen House, where I use expressive writing as a spiritual, self-discovery, and creativity tool for both self-named writers and those who just recognize benefits of writing as a life skill. As a presenter contracted by the local school district, hospital, and other organizations, I have introduced teachers, children, business owners, and others to the mental, emotional, and physical benefits of journaling.

In my blog I write about language and expressive writing and its connection to creativity and spirituality, in particular. Blogging is one aspect of my own TLA practice, for which I also write a journal, where I discover how to truly get out of my own way and make life-changing decisions.

In 2010, wanting to get more "street cred" as a writing-for-well-being facilitator, I began the TLA program at Goddard College. While I was studying, both my workshops and writing took a turn toward spirituality—which I define as the connection between all things, inner and outer—of which expressive writing, I believe, is a direct expression. Such writing allows people to access personal, cultural, and archetypal symbols and metaphors, which not only produce mind-blowingly beautiful and truthful writing, but build self-confidence through self-knowledge and acceptance.

Hearing the sharp intake of breath when a personal truth, written or read, resonates deeply, or listening to the pure poetry that has poured onto the paper from a simple prompt and in only ten minutes—these are the things that make my job the best in the world.

www.wisdomwithinink.com

8

# Women's Self-Leadership through Transformative Narratives

YVETTE ANGELIQUE HYATER-ADAMS

"The world will be saved by Western women," said the Dalai Lama at the Vancouver Peace Summit in 2009 (Chan, 2010). His statement rippled across social media like wild dandelions racing in grassy meadows. Some questioned if the Dalai Lama was overlooking the great achievements of other women in the world. Others wondered if the Dalai Lama was noticing how Western women, who tended to have more access to developing leadership and having influence than some other populations of women, were in a prime position to put into action qualities many women foster in their lives, such as compassion, nurturance, and collaboration.

The number of successful women leaders in the workplace is rapidly growing, and compassionate, nurturing, and collaborative leadership is highly effective and desired among governments, nonprofits, and businesses around the globe (Gerzema and D'Antonio, 2013). If the Dalai Lama is right about Western women saving the world, then it is even more important for women to develop and exercise their leadership potential. Developing such leadership begins with self-leadership: women finding guidance and direction within so that they can lead others.

I am a coach, teacher, and facilitator specializing in women's leadership. I am also one who has found great vitality and guidance through words throughout my life. Thus, I was drawn to creating a model that helps people transform their narratives about who they are and what their work is in the world in order to help women develop their leadership potential.

Thinking back on how much I found in poetry, stories, and guiding metaphors, I discovered multiple ways in which I learned to develop my own leadership skills. For instance, Madeleine L'Engle's children's book *A Wrinkle in Time* (1962) helped me understand there may be dimensions and alternative possibilities not always obvious; Mary Oliver's poem "The Journey" (1986) acknowledged my feelings of wanting to fix what was beyond my scope while guiding me toward where my action could be more effective. These, and many other examples from literature, led to the development of a "transformative narratives" process to help women develop their leadership, which I define in the same way Neck and Manz (2013) do, as the process of influence.

Through reflective and imaginative writing, women can build upon traits associated with the feminine, such as listening, collaboration, and creativity, and use their personal histories, present stories, and future scenarios as a resource. Beginning with self-leadership, which promotes orchestrating a self-directed development journey for authentic leadership, women can better guide themselves, their businesses, and communities.

## Women's Ways of Leading

In the fall of 2013, in a volleying match between President Obama and the U.S. Congress, about 15 percent of the federal government shut down for several weeks in a bipartisan gridlock over the budget. After spending enough time at a standstill, twenty women senators across political lines met for pizza, salad, and wine one evening in one of their offices, and they began to build a bipartisan solution that was eventually introduced to the whole Congress (Newton-Small, 2013). Their efforts reignited negotiations between both parties and resulted in the resolution of the stalemate. Women, pizza, and pinot noir eventually led that 15 percent of the federal government back to work. This example is one of many efforts emerging all over the west, east, north, and south of every continent and community.

Collaboration was key here—and in recent research, other qualities, such as nurturance, also stand out in women's leadership. In a 2012 *Harvard Busi-*

*ness Review* blog, Zenger and Folkman conducted a 360-degree feedback study for more than 7,000 leaders. About 65 percent were men. All were evaluated on sixteen leadership competencies. The researchers conducted their analysis differentiated by gender:

> Most stereotypes would have us believe that female leaders excel at "nurturing" competencies such as developing others and building relationships, and many might put exhibiting integrity and engaging in self-development in that category as well. And in all four cases our data concurred—women did score higher than men. (March 15)

Skills such as building relationships and seeking collaborative solutions are necessary for women and men leading in the workplace and community. Women in the 360-degree feedback study ranked lower than men in the areas of financial acumen and strategic perspective, which is also vital to strong leadership in the business world. There are women who are comfortable with financial data, and there are also many women who are not encouraged to understand the language of finance. Women today need to build upon both relational leadership skills and befriend financial acumen in ways that are meaningful for us.

Lack of women in executive ranks keep organizational eyes on the few "only," and these women receive greater scrutiny in performance versus their male counterparts. Women in Zenger and Folkman's 2012 leadership study made statements such as "We need to work harder than men to prove ourselves," and "We feel the constant pressure to never make a mistake, and to continually prove our value to the organization."

Yet there is also a new story emerging: an overwhelming proportion of women and men in leadership roles see feminine values as key to twenty-first-century leaders. Gerzema and D'Antonio (2013) found ten feminine core traits/values that were necessary for effective leadership: connectedness, humility, candor, patience, empathy, trustworthiness, openness, flexibility, vulnerability, and balance.

For women to foster leadership while embracing such values, they must push themselves and others to explore questions such as *Who am I? What is the well-being I want to see for myself and people around me? How do I facilitate making this happen?* As a coach, I work with women to cultivate and preserve their narratives so that they can express and creatively use their stories of who they are and how they want to lead themselves and others. In the women's coaching circles that I facilitate, women express doubt in their leadership in such statements as

> "I'm not a leader. I just support the work and relationships for my CEO."
> "I'm not a leader. I'm just a mom raising kids."
> "I'm not sure if I'm ready to take my business to the next level."

Women voicing doubts often are balancing dual commitments in the home and at work, which can make it difficult to keep sight of the bigger picture in how they lead change in front of or behind public faces of leadership (Rivkin and Rubin, 2012). Seeing themselves as invisible or silencing their voices isn't a way women can "save" the world or, more importantly, show leadership.

Understanding leadership begins with taking a deep dive into self-awareness through reflection and dialogue. One of the first and most vital steps for women is to dedicate time to develop their leadership potential, and then to start leadership with themselves. It is important for women to bring doubts to the surface and unpack them. In my transformative narrative coaching work, I help women reframe doubtful language into words for possibilities through the power of poetry, stories, and guiding metaphors. A starting process is to invite women to write stories on how they perceive their current state. Inevitably, the story contains language such as "I am really lazy and procrastinate." Together we pull out negative phrases in the story and consider other possibilities at play. When the "story under the story" is fully revealed, a statement like "I am lazy and procrastinate" might be reframed as "I am releasing several commitments to reflect and gain clarity on what I need to do next." Understanding the "why" underneath the judgment of "lazy and procrastinate" is key for women who don't recognize ways they might do too much.

## Transformative Narratives and Self-Leadership

The impetus to create transformative narratives emerged out of my own life experience in using the power of words to break silences, heal, and possibility-solve. Transformative narratives open up channels for me to artistically express my voice through writing poetry, memoir, and essay, while recognizing and using my strengths as a business leader. As a longtime business leader, and a lover of literature, I developed transformative narrative coaching while a graduate student in the Transformative Language Arts program at Goddard College. In the years since my 2003 graduation, I have further developed this approach through working extensively with clients, research, facilitating workshops, and leading retreats. My audience includes all women as well as a few men who welcome feminine-values leadership, which is trending as the leadership model for the twenty-first century.

The transformative narratives process draws from the interdisciplinary studies of creative writing, humanistic and relational cultural theory (RCT) psychology, biblio/poetry therapy, narrative therapy, Buddhist philosophy, and adult learning theories. The theoretical foundations include:

- *Creative writing*: Applying positive feedback methods on writing and stories.
- *Psychology theories:* Relational cultural theory, person-centered therapy, and positive psychology where emphasis is on safety, acknowledgment, and affirming self.
- *Adult learning theory:* Experiential learning and reflection-on-action.
- *Narrative therapy:* Externalizing narratives and separating the person from the "problem" stories.
- *Poetry therapy:* Process for poem and literature selection and use of literature as a catalyst for conversation or intervention (Hynes and Hynes-Berry, 1994).
- *Mindfulness practices:* Laws of cause and effect, meditation, and deep breathing.
- *Scenario planning:* Creating possibility stories.

Synthesizing these concepts is an art in itself. Core components to the transformative narratives model are

- creating a safe container to unearth stories,
- using poetry or other forms of literature to engage the dialogue,
- practicing "narrative listening" (deep listening for the story being told) in hearing others' stories, and
- creating stories for personal change.

When women can recognize their power to choose through creatively revealing, engaging, and building stories from personal history and imagination, both confidence and ability to influence individuals and systems are strengthened.

Emergent research (Neck and Manz, 2013; Norris, 2008) defines self-leadership as the process of influencing oneself. This is an attractive proposition for women because it focuses on leading ourselves before we lead others. In mapping out a self-leadership journey, we first take personal ownership for our development, which entails practicing self-observing, self-goal-setting, and self-accountability. There are plenty of tools and behavioral techniques that can help us develop skills personalized to play to our strengths. For example, instead of producing a top-down "to-do" list, one might create a series of "thought bubbles" as a schema, less linear in its format. In Neck and Manz's self-leadership model, redesigning our mental approaches, outcomes, and behaviors allow us to improve personal effectiveness.

Self-leadership emphasizes a person identifying his or her thinking patterns and choosing the best options as the first step toward leading others effectively. For example, my clearest thinking is enhanced by shutting down my access to the Internet to avoid distraction and by listening to Bach's Baroque music to help concentration. Paying attention to thinking patterns and subsequent choices helps people strengthen their trust of their own voice, intuition, and self-knowledge.

Respecting the perspective articulated by thought leaders Neck and Manz, I posit there is a nuance that makes self-leadership for women different than for men. It has to do with how a woman shapes her sense of self. In 1976, Jean Baker Miller wrote *Toward a New Psychology of Women*, a groundbreaking book told in an engaging narrative voice. Miller reveals practical ways women develop a sense of self, but she also takes into account issues of difference and power, particularly by race, class, and sexual orientation, acknowledging other diversities. Miller and her colleagues later built the theoretical framework Relational-Cultural Theory (RCT) as a model for working with women in a psychological context (Miller and Stiver, 1997). Janet L. Surrey, one of the founding scholars in RCT, states, "Our conception of the self-in-relation involves the recognition that, for women, the primary experience of self is relational; that is, the self is organized and developed in the context of important relationships" (1985, paper 13).

This assertion proves true from my experience when coaching women developing their leadership competency. In the Business and Entrepreneurship for Creatives class I teach, women experienced positive outcomes when working individually and in relationship with others. Sharing stories in one-on-one sessions or even small groups of five to seven people creates synergy among the women involved and helps them find great clarity in their direction forward. When women gain clarity on where they are heading, and have a narrative picture of how it looks, it builds confidence and strengthens a woman's ability to take action and achieve goals.

In providing leadership coaching to women and men, I notice differences in how each social identity group handles choice. For example, I sometimes find that women of color expect to deal with whatever decisions are handed to them without believing they're entitled to make their own choices. Some people of color and women may wrestle with "self" premises in the self-leadership model because it may feel culturally counterintuitive. How might women in self-leadership explore "self" when it might mean including others? These are complex issues and questions that need innovative solutions, such as are found through reading and/or writing about images and metaphors found in literature.

The complexity of self-leadership for women needs additional exploration. Neck and Manz's model offers a powerful perspective for leadership development, yet it dances along some traditional values associated with male traits that could perpetuate assumptions and practices favoring privileged groups. Women and people of color cannot assume equal access, equal paths, or equal support when navigating a personal choice approach as dictated by the self-leadership model. I want to see women acknowledge, embrace, and work through our cultural and silencing stories as a self-awareness method. Taking the next step entails these stories, revealing our strength and leadership capabilities.

## Using Poetry and Stories for Self-Leadership

Unpacking women's stories and examining women's personal and social identity group histories can help shed light on their understanding of authentic self-development. Creating scenarios, making clear choices, and adapting to change are critical leadership skills, all of which can be done through the transformative narrative process. Reading and relating to literature, along with writing and telling our stories, is a way to develop sense-making skills essential to effective leadership. This is particularly important because not all women have equal access to or have financial resources for professional training, coaching, or higher education. From college students to CEOs, the women I work with using transformative narratives eventually come to realize the significance of their experience, brilliance, and potential. Women often overlook or are unaware of their own talents. Mapping out a self-leadership learning journey using transformative narratives can be a successful formula for women to meet leadership development goals.

When supporting women in designing self-leadership journeys, I share stories of real and imagined characters in literature as a way to expand mindsets on what is possible. Harvard Business School's Joseph Badaracco (2006) writes about leadership and literature and argues that serious literature, such as Arthur Miller's *Death of a Salesman* or Joseph Conrad's *Secret Sharer*, can give glimpses from inside of a character that may live in thoughts and feelings of a leader. In William Ayot's (2007) poem "The Contract: A Word from the Led," the narrator speaks from the voice of followers who acknowledge the complexity leaders face—and at the same time expect leaders to stay true. This poem offers recognition of the significance of *being authentic* as a leader. These "literary mentors" can be a helpful resource for envisioning effective leadership. At the same time, women need to unpack "truths" about themselves, and this starts with deep self-awareness work. We must each begin by doing our own inner work.

Sometimes women leaders are unsure where to begin self-awareness work. A journal is an excellent personal reflection tool and container for capturing key learning. I often suggest that a self-awareness journal begin with this statement: "Today, I, (name of individual), begin telling myself the truth." This simple phrase can open fiercely harbored secrets and unconsciously held stories. The work of self-awareness is to reveal the story that needs to be told.

Women can learn about risk, courage, and taking personal action through poetry, such as that by the inspirational Lucille Clifton. She often shows us in her poems the essence of a moment, decision, or personal awareness. Recently, a business owner of a midsize firm discussed how she didn't have the right business "status" to ask certain leaders with greater resources to become a part of her personal board of directors. Working deeply with Clifton's poem "it was a dream" (1993), in which the poet's "greater self" tells her that "This. This. This" is what can be done in the face of professed helplessness, we came up with a "*This* List," where my client detailed her main courses of action. Clifton makes inferences in the poem of what she could have done differently; my client followed her lead and articulated them. From the *This* List we created *possibility stories* in painting a narrative portrait of her success in getting what she needed from others outside her social status. She took a risk and began living the story. She received some unexpected "yes" responses.

The transformative narratives process is a creative, storytelling-based approach to personal development in which making personal connections to literature is a powerful tool. Poetry, flash nonfiction (very short stories people can write or read), and short essays can be used as catalysts to elicit personal histories, inspire visioning, and help reveal leadership success stories (Hyater-Adams, 2010; 2012). Women begin to apply success stories from the past to new situations and identify additional strategies to help meet goals. For example, a woman might remember she trained for a 5K walk every morning in relentless sun, freezing rain, and snow, offering proof she can be disciplined and dedicated to a task and achieve goals. I find that women can more readily embody useful strategies when framed as stories.

Last summer, I used the transformative narratives process with a group of small business leaders, all women, who were looking to enhance their leadership skills and take their businesses to the next level. I used Lucille Clifton's poem "Climbing" (1993), which includes a metaphor for naming any personal and societal struggles that get in the way of achieving goals. At the end of the poem, Clifton speaks reflectively and wonders if, in her journey, she should have desired more; even though she is climbing a rope behind another woman, she notices the other woman passes sixty years in her climbing. Clifton describes her fatigue, but she still continues, elevating herself up the rope. She doesn't tire and never gives up.

I invited the class participants, women aged fifty to sixty-five, with one in her twenties, to first explore the poem by reflecting back words and images that resonated and lingered with them. Some women liked the images and the tenacity of the poet, reaching sixty and still climbing. The women in the class saw themselves as viable leaders in business and in their communities. They reported that the poem inspired them to forge forward. The women were guided into deeper exploration with a writing exercise:

> Growing a business is like facing a long rope and preparing for the climb. To succeed is to *believe in* and be the business you imagine. Our task is to be able to talk about our work with clarity, authenticity, and succinctness. Imagine having the business you've longed for. . . . Write with explicit detail what you are doing and how you are being as the leader of your business. As you lift yourself up, what are you ready to let go of to grow the business you've longed for?

Women in the group veered into amazing places. Some women discovered feeling as if they were "taking up too much space," and this feeling stopped them from expanding their businesses. One example shared how it didn't feel "nice" to sell her services in yoga or massage therapy (because everyone should have access to this) and it felt strange to compete with other like services. Two women realized they had to let go of saying "yes" to every request, which kept them from having time to care for themselves. Another woman admitted she needed to get out of her current management consulting business and do something different. All of this began as reflective writing on specific questions related to the poem, followed by sharing our reflections.

Women in the class began taking responsibility for making changes to align with their life purpose. We met on alternate Fridays, so the women initiated meetings in between classroom time in duos and trios to move further their individual plans. The women consistently reported how well they moved forward with their individual plans. They worked on their respective business plans, exchanged feedback, and encouraged each other to take risks. They reported how the course was a holistic approach to growing their businesses.

People remember stories that create clear action. During the five classroom sessions, the participants created a series of stories that reflected clear actions. As the group's coach, I helped them sort through which stories were important to support their journey, explore missing narratives, unearth new stories, and release any stories created that no longer served them. The format of the story can be of any genre or length—a poem or short story, a few pages or just six words, modeled after SMITH Magazine's mini-memoir project.[1] Stories of any length are a source of our creativity and voice the many ways we hear ourselves. When participants in my class wrote a variety of stories inspiring them to take action, they felt as though they had a concrete map on how to move forward. After completing the five classes, I met with each participant one-on-one for a coaching session to help each woman embody her new story.

Six months after the end of the program, one participant was making big, noticeable strides. She aggressively pursued her plan as an artistic photographer. She entered several shows and placed first in two categories and second in a juried photography show. She increased sales for her artwork. Having a clear purpose, mapping out a self-directed journey, and taking a chance on herself are paying results in this woman's life and on-purpose leadership.

## Self-Leadership Begins and Ends with Us

As a writer, coach, and facilitator, I constantly learn from my students and clients and, most of all, from my own journey into evolving self-leadership. Using the transformative narrative process myself to clarify developing goals and apparent obstacles and ways to navigate around those obstacles, I often examine my own guiding narrative to ensure that it matches where I am being led next in my work and life.

I close this chapter with an excerpt of a vision story I wrote in 2003 with my transformative narrative coaching circle. This example of a typical day in the realized life, a writing prompt I give to clients and also assigned to myself, demonstrates how a powerful story can be embodied and executed at a deep level. While I was working on helping my clients develop their leadership, I also found more of the work I was called to lead. The best part of this story for me is how 80 percent of it came to fruition—I'm still working on the wraparound porch.

> The willow tree reaches for the rail of the white wraparound porch. *This place must be 100 years old.* I stand back and take in a whole view. In all of its oldness, it is perfect. Walking in the front door, I notice framed letters litter the hallway walls—testimonial stories from others before me, describing how wonderful their experience and the significant changes happening in their lives.
>
> My heart is heavy at not being where I need to be. Saying "yes" to every assignment should have landed me the division head position. But is that what I really want? I feel as though I've lost my way. *What are my interests? What are all of my talents? What do I want? Who am I?*

So I've taken charge of my leadership development. I'm working with a coach and peer group where we're writing and talking—it's called transformative narratives for leaders. It pushes me to put thoughts, feelings, and dreams to paper. I am getting clear and carving out a direction. Using poems and flash nonfiction as teachers stopped feeling strange after the third session. Poetry and short prose act as a catalyst for deepening my learning. The encouragement and support from my coach and peer group is a great help.

This is *a magical place*. It's warm and welcoming, feels like home. The willow tree and country porch is a big hug and safe place to contemplate what's essential for my personal growth. There is no judgment or blame here—just personal truth telling and revealing the authentic leader that lives in me.

## Note

1. The origin of the "six-word memoir" is attributed to Ernest Hemingway, who reportedly wrote an entire story in six words: *For sale. Baby shoes. Never worn.*

## References

Ayot, William. 2007. The contract: A word from the led. In *Leading from within: Poetry that sustains the courage to lead*, eds. S. M. Intrator and M. Scribner. San Francisco: Jossey-Bass.

Badaracco, Joseph, Jr. 2006. *Questions of character: Illuminating the heart of leadership through literature.* Boston: Harvard Business School.

Chan, Victor. 2010. Western women can come to the rescue of the world. The Dalai Lama Center. January 25. http://dalailamacenter.org/blog-post/western-women-can-come-rescue-world.

Clifton, Lucille. 1993. *The book of light.* Port Townsend, WA: Copper Canyon.

Gerzema, John, and Michael D'Antonio. 2013. *The Athena doctrine: How women (and the men who think like them) will rule the future.* San Francisco: Jossey-Bass

Hyater-Adams, Yvette A. 2010. Learning diversity and leadership skills through transformative narratives. *Tamara Journal of Critical Inquiry*, 8:208–32.

——. 2012. How to get going with personal narrative in scholarly writing. *Practicing Social Change*, 5:38–41.

Hynes, Arlene McCarty, and Mary Hynes-Berry. 1994. *Biblio/poetry therapy: The interactive process: A handbook*. St. Cloud, MN: North Star.

L'Engle, Madeline. 1962. *A wrinkle in time*. New York: Farrar, Straus and Giroux.

Miller, Jean Baker. 1976. *Toward a new psychology of women*. Kindle edition. Boston: Beacon.

Miller, Jean Baker, and Irene Pierce Stiver. 1997. *The healing connection: How women form relationships in therapy and life*. Boston: Beacon.

Neck, Christopher P., and Charles C. Manz. 2013. *Mastering self-leadership: Empowering yourself for personal excellence*, 6th ed. Kindle edition. Upper Saddle River, NJ: Pearson.

Newton-Small, Jay. 2013. Women are the only adults left in Washington. *Time*, October 16. http://swampland.time.com/2013/10/16/women-are-the-only-adults-left-in-washington/ (accessed January 15, 2014).

Norris, Sharon E. 2008. An examination of self-leadership. *Emerging Leadership Journeys*, 2:43–61.

Oliver, Mary. 1986. The journey. In *Dream work*. New York: Atlantic Monthly Press.

Rivkin, Rosalyn, and Sally Park Rubin. 2012. *The overfunctioning woman's handbook*. Kindle edition. Orinda, CA: Park Rubin Media.

SMITH Magazine. *Six Words*. http://sixwordmemoirs.com (accessed May 2, 2014).

Surrey, Janet L. 1985. The "self-in-relation": A theory of women's development. Paper no. 13 in a self-published series.

Zenger, Jack, and Joseph Folkman. 2012. Are women better leaders than men? *HBR* Blog Network. March 15. http://blogs.hbr.org/2012/03/a-study-in-leadership-women-do/ (accessed May 2, 2014).

# *Snapshot*

## Lisa McIvor, Seattle, Washington

*Home health nurse, workshop facilitator for people with disabilities, poet and writer*

As a poet, I have personally found much healing through my writing. This is the place my joy in this emerging field begins, where I can rediscover my own voice, finding the spaciousness to move from that understanding forward. Initially I was not sure how this work could be connected directly to my work as a home health nurse. However, through my graduate study practicum, the practice of transformative language arts has been integrated into my current profession with an ease that continues to amaze me.

For the past twenty-four years I have worked with Provail, formerly known as Cerebral Palsy Association of King/Snohomish County, a nonprofit agency that helps individuals living with disabilities to live as full and independent lives as possible. Five years ago, the agency developed a program, "Art Is Not an Option," which meets monthly at a local art studio and focuses first only on painting. When I approached our art director with the idea of a writing group, she was very supportive, and so began "A Journey of Words Poetry Circle."

One aspect of the group I had not originally anticipated was the enthusiasm shown by the support staff who participate. Two speech therapists often help members of the group who are nonverbal, or who use a DynaVox or LightTalker device to communicate. As most everyone uses an electric wheelchair and has needs for daily care, I invited each person's caregiver to attend. In the relationship between caregiver and client, there is always a sense of necessary professional boundaries that are important, but in this circle our words were equal and provided an avenue of connection and trust that felt as natural as breathing. Now our group is eager to attend some literary events in and around Seattle in the coming year.

This is what I really love about the practice of TLA—how the artistic medium of language provides both a safe container for the work of individual healing and wellness and allows for the creation of trust and co-creation within community. Through our words we heal, through the sharing of these words, we heal together.

www.artisnotanoption.wordpress.com

# *Snapshot*

## Jen Cross, Oakland, California

*Writer and erotic writer, facilitator of workshops for survivors of sexual violence and for erotic writing*

Photo by Sarah Deragon, Portraits to the People

I journal every day as a matter of maintenance, meditation, self-care, and play. My daily writing practice feels like an integral part of my transformative language arts practice. I also write for publication—on my blog and elsewhere—about living and writing in the aftermath of sexual trauma, erotic writing as liberatory practice, writing as a tool of transformation for trauma survivors, and more.

I write about sex as a means of survival and reclamation. As a queer woman who is a sexual abuse survivor, I've used writing to undermine stereotypes and reconnect with my sexuality, desire, and sense of embodiment. I write about sex because it's fun, because it's a powerful way for me to learn about my characters, and because sex continues to be a site of oppression and stereotyping in our culture. I write characters who have complicated sexualities, making room in the world for my erotic experience and that of many in my communities to replace the cultural stories feeding us the idea our wounds forever make us damaged.

For more than ten years I've facilitated transformative writing workshops and groups in the San Francisco Bay Area on surviving trauma, erotic writing, manuscript development, and general-topic groups. I believe in not focusing all our writing on our trauma stories, but instead on our desire now, giving us the opportunity to experience ourselves as creative and desiring beings first, and survivors second.

There's so much I love about this work: the connection that happens among writers in a group, especially in a group of trauma survivors. Often it happens that a participant has written something they disclaim the hell out of, dismissing it before they've even shared the words. Then they read their new writing, and it leaves us all breathless. We are in awe of the risks that the writer took in the work, or the way she managed to language something new, or the willingness to find words for something that hadn't been spoken ever before, or simply the striking beauty of the piece. In hearing our experiences mirrored in the writing of others, we let crumble a piece of the wall that our abusers forced us to build within ourselves in order to survive.

I also get to bear witness to folks' transformation through writing. People who, early on, were barely willing to read their writing aloud to the group might find themselves, just a few months later, standing before a packed audience to perform their work, or changing their lives to invite in regular creative expression, and making lasting connections with peers. I've seen people, through their writing, cultivate the strength to leave difficult relationships, confront family members, seek more satisfying work, and more fully inhabit their voices and lives. I get to witness writers who could barely get words on the page transform into folks whose pens won't quit.

And I love getting to write and read others' writing for a living!

www.writingourselveswhole.org

# Snapshot

## Angie River, Port Angeles, Washington

*Spoken-word and burlesque artist*

My performances tell a piece of my story. My hope is that through those stories, the audience can see an aspect of their own story and feel inspired to tell their stories. In my community and surrounding communities, I perform in and produce various multigenre performances, ranging from spoken-word poetry, to poetic monologues, to modern dance, to burlesque. The focus of many of my performances is the body—and being a woman. One of my favorite performance pieces, "Squishy List," includes quotes from women friends about the way they saw their bodies as children, a theatrical dialogue based on a conversation about bodies between me and my young daughter, then a mock-burlesque performance about all the squishy parts of my body.

As an introvert and a people-watcher, I observe people, watching the different ways they tell their stories without words, listening to how they tell their stories with words. I have seen the transformative power that comes just from uttering your truth, and I have always believed in the healing nature of creativity. I personally have found performing my truths and exposing my stories to be incredibly empowering, and I hope to share that with others.

We often feel so alone and disconnected, but what I've found is that through these performances I feel connected to the audience, the audience feels connected to me and other performers, and, most of all, to their true selves. Honestly, what happens at these performances can be life-altering.

Facebook: under "Rebel on Stage"

9

# Autobiography of a Social Body

JULIANA BORRERO

> I like the scar, the story.
>
> —*Cixous (1994, 16)*
>
> It is the other who makes my portrait.
>
> —*Cixous (1994, 13)*

*Note to the reader: This chapter seeks to engage you in the experience of listening to the other's story, inviting you to take part in the utopian and limitless project of autobiography as a collective exercise between tellers and listeners, which promises to bring together the broken and silenced pieces that we are, recognizing and reconstructing our part within the social body. Inspired by Virginia Woolf's novel* The Waves*—a story told by multiple voices, where the diversity, beauty, and fragility of the human condition and its strong umbilical cord to language awake in us a renewed sense of what it means to be alive—this chapter takes the form of ripples in a pond, a collection of resonances that rhythmically echoes and unfolds between autobiographical fragments from the young Colombian writers in the Language and Peace Project, the poetic/academic reflections of the author, discussions of supporting theorists, and studies of literary works. This chapter is also shaped like the Language and Peace group itself—in its fluctuating, rippling, echoing way of putting ideas together, it carries the multiple, amorous, organic rhythm of our weekly meetings. In* *these ways, as they ponder the reconstruction of our ailing social body through language, these pages literally weave together a patched "textual body" where "high" and "low" knowledge, poetry and thought, daily life stories and literary works, academic and political reflection coexist.*

Finally, the missing link: How does this invitation to reconstruct the social body coming from the south face of the Americas send (and receive) ripples to (and from) the reader in the north face? How may this tendency for reconstruction through language spread through the surface of the Americas, echoing, resonating, learning from differences and reconstructing our limits and possibilities as a greater social body? This is up to all of us.

This chapter is the reconstruction of a chapter in a literary research project called Language and Peace, set in a university in rural Colombia—its dream, its participants, its theoretical and literary allies; and of a method, collective autobiography—that we applied according to our own rules of the game and experimented with extensively over a set of years. Its pages are interspersed with samples of the intimate, fragile, autobiographical writing practiced in the group that we used in order to study the nation's violence. These years of collective autobiographical exploration set those of us who were a part of it on a radically divergent road, one that led us to understand work with literature as a practice of discovery, sensitivity, and active work on ourselves and others that is a radical form of ethics: a literature oriented towards the formation of people, rather than to the analysis of literary works.

Before I begin my story, though, I want to talk about the difficulties of working on this divergent road. In the midst of a traditional academic setting, attention to the words and stories of the other, the sincere passion for the minute and particular stories of human beings, the slow work of allowing the conditions for these stories to be told and processed, and their role in the healing and building of communities, does not seem to be of interest. This kind of work is seen as too personal, irrelevant, unaesthetic or lacking abstraction and cognitive depth that is "characteristic" of academia. Because this line of work, its concerns and its narratives, are constantly being rejected—in academic journals, as curricular guidelines, as thesis projects, or foci of student interest—one struggles to find allies in other disciplines, in interdisciplinary or "in-disciplined" spaces.

Embodiment studies, mixed with snippets of poststructuralist theory, women's studies and contemporary art theory have provided the theoretical foundation for the Language and Peace Project's understanding of language. Transformative language arts—and its lively interdisciplinary blend of psychologists, social workers, pedagogues, artists, and others, all of them powerful writers—has been our most meaningful ally in proposing literature as a form of political and social action in the academic setting. Through these connections, we legitimately/illegitimately step over the boundaries of our disciplines and reach out, seek dialogue, collaborate, redefine. In this process, it begins to seem possible to envision a different sort of knowledge system, with a different sort of community.

## The Project

The Language and Peace Project started ten years ago as a utopian collective adventure to propose a practice of literature that would contribute to the formation of a culture of peace. In the context of our ailing, war-ridden country, our dream was to set in motion the powerful words of Christa Wolf: "Today, literature must be peace research . . . literature should be allowed to draw its own map, to counteract those maps of death and destruction that surround us" (1995, 177). Traditionally, literature and the arts have been defined as that kind of work that has no purpose, that is not inscribed in a system of use; nevertheless we wanted to give literature a reason for being, to put it to work in our broken world. Alongside transformative language arts, we worked from the conviction that words are powerful, that they have the power to change our lives and others', and the conviction that literature and the arts have a role and a responsibility in social and personal transformation, which allow us to make contact with others and participate in the construction of our communities (Mirriam-Goldberg and Tallman, 2007, 10–12).

In addition to this quest for the purpose of literature, it concerned us that language seemed to have become a stereotype and lost its power (Barthes, 1975, 42) in a world where it was so ardently needed. Urged by the anger and helplessness of not knowing what was our place in the social mesh of violence called "nation," we began searching for what we called "a language of desire." Our bet was that reconceptualizing language in relation to desire implied rethinking its relation with the human subjects that we were; listening to the rhythms of our bodies, our hopes and fears, our contradictions, our changeability; recognizing our particularity, understanding our differences, and reconstructing our daily, invisible, unheard stories. That is how we arrived at the topic of autobiography.

We framed autobiography as the recovery of the self as open question, the self in constant movement, transformation, invention. Autobiography was the possibility of asking ourselves about the implications of the absence of the subject position in knowledge, and of discovering the other, not as usurper, but as the one who questions and completes my own story. Our work allowed us to experience autobiography as stance, more than as literary genre: It was a form of thinking and human interrelation, a mirror of nation, and space for reconstruction of the word "peace."

But one of the rules of the game at the Language and Peace Project has been that theory should not be separated from practice, or thinking from the act of creating and creating one's self. In order to achieve this exploration of the self as contradiction and changeability we used "writing from the body." This technique adds depth, play, rhythm to autobiography and enables this study of the self as movement and open question.

What does it mean to write from the body? This is Hélène Cixous' passionately poetic orientation:

> I don't "begin" by "writing," I don't write. Life becomes text starting from my body. I am already text. History, love, violence, time, work, desire inscribe it in my body. . . .Vision: my breast as the Tabernacle. Open. My lungs like the scrolls of the Torah, but a Torah without end whose scrolls are imprinted and unfurled throughout time, and in the same History, all the histories, events, ephemeral changes and transformations are written, I enter into myself with my eyes closed and you can read it. This reading is performed here, by the being-who-wants-to-be-born, by an urge, something that wants at all costs to come out, to be exhaled, . . . a force that contracts the muscles of my womb and stretches my diaphragm as if I were about to give birth or to come. And it's the same thing. (1991, 52)

Writing from the body comes from the "life" inscribed in our conscious but especially unconscious bodily experience. History, experience, potency . . . are all there, body. But it is necessary to close our eyes in order to see them and hear their narrative. Writing is a way of knowing that involves not knowing as orientation. It is a practice of attention to our urgent and unanswered questions, contradictions, rhythms, dreams, fears, pleasures, vibrations that reveal unconscious knowledge about who we are and what we are experiencing, and it implies inventing ourselves over and over again as many times as our constantly changing bodies demand it. Our work at the Language and Peace Project has been that of taking literature to the bodies that we are, and the body—the complexity of its experience—again, to literature. This is a risky journey that involves a ripping of veils, a cracking of the voice, multiple reconstructions of self, and the possibility of encountering a blue flower of hope along the way.

This chapter is dedicated to my students Adela Ávila González, Jasbleidi Rocío Gavilán Castro, Angélica María López, Libardo Cortés, Carolina Peña, Gloria Inés González, Andrea Paola Vargas Quiroz, Mauricio Urrea, and co-researcher Juan Carlos Silva, whose voices are present in this text, and whose courage and persistence to believe in roads of language that opened ways of life, reconfigured the boundaries of my world, and allowed me to redimension what work with language could be.

**Loose Limbs**

*Chopping the onion of identity* *I chopped off my finger*
Arms without claws coming out from under the bed *Exploring the body*
I touch a scar
t h e r e f l e c t i o n o n t h e m i r r o r i s n o t r e a l i t y A
sea that does not speak clearly
*My eyes touch you* *hurting and smelling* *my 13 ambitions* We
lose the freedom of sex We bite the lips of silence
*Water is my path* a n d g l a s s i s m y f e a r . . .
Fragments of a larger body, we are . . .

I want to write about the Language and Peace group as body, our weekly work as that of becoming part of a body, knowing that there is an *us* that stretches down the paths of my days like a piece of rubber. I am only part of this body that constitutes the group, but it holds me together. The vertigo, the uncertainty, the slow gathering of a rhythm in collective work. How I slowly let my self be known, gaze by gaze and gesture by gesture. We begin descending steps inside our selves and now we must invent a tongue that allows us to be faithful to our desire. It is not that difference is suppressed, but rather that I start knowing the other's terrain, with its fenced-in horses and its luminous sectors. Each word unfolds like a fan of meaning, with its own weight, its own story. And my tongue is both more and less mine. My tongue is her ear. My mouth is her stomach.

## Listening

> There was a car. The rain was falling hard. I could barely see ahead of us. I was afraid that we would not make it. They gave me money, but it was not what I expected. I felt that all their eyes were on me. My eyes evading the rear-view mirror, not wanting to meet theirs. I felt the knives of fear. I felt the tears that wanted to come out of me like the rain. I knew I wanted something else, somewhere else. I finally was able to part ways. Only then could I cry. (Ulloa, in Ávila, Cortés et al., 2005)

"We who are a wound by the other, of the other, for the other" (Cixous, 1994, 86). I want to talk about the other; so many others talk about the other . . . we make it the principal pawn of our discourse. But who is the other, and how to ensure that his/her meaning does not become abstract and diffuse like so many other theoretical key words? How does the idea of other alter from person to person? How does it respond to the shape of each body? How does the story of the other shed light upon the story of each one?

> I remember the blush of the deer's sun[1] behind the street signs that led to the old airport in the afternoons at Atamaica, the farm where I grew up. In the morning, coming back from the river, after my morning bath, I liked to contemplate the first rays of sun peeping through the dance of myrtle and *mortesino* trees that awoke to the sound of the summer breeze and the hullabaloo of birds. It is difficult and inevitable for me to speak about Atamaica and the horror of four consecutive generations that constitute my family, but in that moment I was an ordinary country boy. We lived in three large houses but they looked like only one from the outside, with their abobe and *bahareque*[2] walls and *moriche* palm roof. At the entrance, we were welcomed by a sleeping dog under jasmine and red cayena flowers. I still have the scars on my hands from sharpening the machetes at the *marmaja* stone close to the *water well*, and I remember the stories of Uncle Rabbit,[3] the Fireball,[4] and the Whistler,[5] that father told us at night, at the same time as he taught us that

> the time to plant was in August during full moon and the time to cut wood was when the moon was waning. But my most intense memory is the juice of the *paraguay* plant; I can still taste the thick green juice of that herb that grew in the garden and that we had to drink every so often for protection against malaria. (Cortés, in Ávila, Cortés et al., 2005)

Bakhtin (1986) speaks about the search for the living word, where the act of enunciation does not end in the speaker but rather in the listener; where the destination of enunciation is the other; where each word finds its true significance not in the original intention of the speaker but in the other's response. Dialogism versus a monological system of knowledge. What would it mean to practice dialogism? How can we feel and access the world of the other?

> My father didn't let us go near this hole he had in the back of the house. It was called. . . . Yes, that's it, a septic pit. . . . There was no water in the neighborhood when I was little. We played and played. There was a pear tree some houses away and my brothers would climb up to steal pears. And in the lot next door, there were pea and corn plants and lots of buried dogs. The neighbor had blue eyes, and I don't know why, they said he had evil eye, and every animal he set his eyes upon died. So they were all there, buried in his back yard. A block away lived a friend of my father who had some kind of back problem; he would come to our house and my father would shave him. (Vargas, in Ávila, Cortés et al., 2005)

The patient and moving work of listening to the other. Every story is immensely important, every story has so much to tell us if only we do not impose on it our idea of what a story should be, what is a protagonist, and which stories deserve to be told.

Asked by academics what was his methodology for producing such wonderful books of testimonial stories on the social processes of the Llanos region of Colombia, Alfredo Molano responds: "I don't follow a strict historical method, I listen to people. I fall in love with their stories" (Molano, 2010, 3–4).

> "Where is he? Let's invite him in for a conference."
> "Nobody knows where he is. He's received threats from the paramilitaries."

## Soiled Stories

> My parents and grandparents have always had rose gardens. Our house was always full of plants. Two bedrooms, one for the parents and one for the children. There are ten of us, three per bed, and they are not all as small as I am. And the kitchen was really small. We had to sit on the floor in order to all fit, it was fun. When we were kids my father would have us picking potatoes in the neighbors' fields. He would come around to check how we were doing and when we accidentally chopped the potatoes he would yell at us in front of everybody. Kafka's father used irony in language. My father just beat us. But there were ways to hide the chopped potatoes, we would just roll them back in the dirt, so no one would notice. He would also scold us when we couldn't lift the heavy half-full potato sacks. So we had to learn to carry them. (Gavilán, in Ávila, Cortés et al., 2005)

One must get soiled with the other's story. We have seen educated shoulders flinch, backs tense, and mouths grimace as they feel that these words are too full of grime, these landscapes too deviant from what is considered beautiful, these characters too insignificant, this discourse too unfit for academic heights. We have seen aggression arise as their hygienic sense of language is questioned, their abstract idea of the other begins to crack. In this country we have sayings like: *"dirty clothes are washed at home," "dirt must be hidden behind the door"*. . . *So why are you bringing it out?* they ask. Shame!

The image of poverty. Dark-skinned children with big bellies walking barefoot by a scandalously beautiful river bed. How to counteract the favorite stereotype of the "third world"? Only with the shape of our faces, the pitch of our voices. There is no shame in the dirt of these stories. Guillermo Páramo, a great Colombian anthropologist and humanist thinker, says that the tragedy of our "peripheral modernity" is that we do not see beauty in our own faces (2001, 2). He speaks of the tribes in the Amazon. Measured in economic terms they would be the farthest behind on the scale of progress. Their homes, not bursting with store-bought furniture, appliances, clothing, paper, and decorations. No bank accounts. No wallet full of credit cards and junk. And yet, in their cosmogony, they consider themselves to be at the umbilicus of the world. How to counteract the havoc of the race of progress? Only with the beauty that is present. Only with forms of knowledge that are rooted in our belly button, and the understanding that reality is much more complex.

> The lover I will give myself to must understand the fear of tying one's shoes. Trembling, with the laces in both hands not knowing which went under and which went over. Trembling because my mother had cut my sister's and my hair—just a little bit—and my father didn't like her to cut our hair. She was such a soft and sweet thing; she was never that way again after she came back from the sanatorium. We were in the house playing when we heard his steps. We could tell from the smell that he was drunk. The first thing he asked was who *cut your hair*. We heard him climb the stairs to my mother's room. We listened in dread. That day he didn't hit her. That day. (González, in Ávila, Cortés et al., 2005)

It would seem that the first word almost always was pain. After the first person was able to say it, more and more pain stained the pages. How many women need to be beaten, how many girls need to be violated, to make a normal family? This kind of work seems to be even harder for the boys. What kind of scars does violence leave in language? What kind of scars are left in silence? As the stories started coming, more and more it seemed that we were walking on a language of eggshells.

> And the grownups told us stories: *La Llorona*,[6] *La Patasola*,[7] appeared to us in the forest where we went when our parents gave us an hour to rest after lunch. We would walk to the forest, then one of us would see the ghosts and run back home. I had dreams of men with dog heads at night. And in front of the house there was an acacia and a pine tree, and we climb on the branches of the acacia and sit, open legged, bouncing up and down, and playing that we were witches on brooms (Gavilán, in Ávila, Cortés et al., 2005).

We think that community can only come when its thinking is rooted in our bodies and the specific forms of our experience: when it responds to our changing stories, our rhythms, our silences, fears, and desires. Only then is there honesty in language. But, what to do if my honest language is wound for one and pleasure for another? What kind of community would result from this honest language of desire? From a language that takes root in real persons?

## Building a House

We follow the path of Heidegger's apparently simple words: "Language is the House of Being" (1971). We are always building our house in language; the question is, "What kind of House have we made for our Selves, and kind of a House do we want to live in? How does this determination affect our language?"

> When I think of owls I think of the infernal sound of the washing machine, and a woman waving a red rag to scare them out of the house. I think of my mother, stirring her coffee with her finger, her hair over her face to hide that she has been crying. I think of my own hysterical fear of moths and mice and owls. "Mama," I want to scream, but my voice dries up. I think about the woman I am becoming, my impurity, my night cries; a little naïve, a little naked, insatiable, disobedient, and wayward. Possessed? With this immense feeling bubbling inside. Tired of all the clandestine sex, oceans of desire. I want to break the window and escape, flying, into the night. Owl woman. How I hate and desire her! (Peña, in Ávila, Cortés et al., 2005)

This kind of writing is not without consequences. Notebooks began to be filled. More and more risks were taken on the pages. Families began to be shaken. Mothers and fathers began to discover or refuse to discover the worlds of their daughters and sons. Notebooks were hidden, thrown out, and burned in wood ovens. Lovers were in shock to "discover" their loved ones. Attachments were cut. Relations had to readjust. Rooms of one's own were sought. Because Language is not decorative, it becomes a life construction, actual work on the bodies that we are.

Language is a House for becoming our Selves. Now that we know this, we are called to participate in its building, because the House that we had lived in was like a prison, or there was no space for us, or we were homeless. We are building a big House with large empty spaces and a river singing next to it; where many others who didn't have a House will be welcome.

### Fine Print

> Will I be able to go through all the darkness? Will writing pull me out in the end? Yes, there is more I have not told you. It is something I have never told anyone. I can't even say it . . . yes, I guess there are many others that have this

> story. I don't know how many Colombian women are holding back this very same . . . You see, when I wrote of demonic characters coming through the window to have sex with me, it was not just a taste for the Gothic. When I write about myself in relation to muck, grime, excrement, I am not lying. You see, my brothers . . . since I was seven . . . I need to write to clean myself of this. I hate them so much and the worst thing is I have to live with them. (Ávila, in Ávila, Cortés et al., 2005)

Being close to this kind of intense sincerity in writing and speaking, several considerations come up with respect to autobiography and exposure, particularly in the Colombian context, where *"dirty clothes must be washed at home"* and *"grime is swept behind the door."* Our culture teaches that "decency," "adequacy" (plus a whole set of other "correct" values) are based on "respect" for the "set-in-stone" boundary between the public and the private. Autobiography is considered an attack on this (moral) (and political) division; *"if these stories have been kept private for so long, there must be a reason"* is the predominant attitude. In a Catholic community such as that of the small rural city where we operate, the validated space for talking about the self is that of "confession," with the morality of those words being judged by a priest. Talking and thinking about oneself in other spaces is considered pretentious; anything different from self-annulment and political conformism is a sign of egocentrism, and even more so if the author of those words is woman or dark-skinned or comes from a rural or working class background. Besides (here comes the next argument), *"Autobiography does not have the same aesthetic value as literature because it is simple and self-referential."*

It is amazing that after all the marvelously complex and critical frameworks that have been done by authors such as Linda Anderson (2001), Paul de Man (2001), Silvia Molloy (1996), Jill Ker Conway (1999), Gloria Anzaldúa (1999), Hélène Cixous (1994), Roland Barthes (1977), Jacques Derrida (Derrida and Bennington, 1993), and others, it is still a battle to propose autobiography as part of the literature curriculum and research at the university where I work. Autobiography is a threat to the story we have been told to believe about who we are and what is our (non)place in nation. Autobiography puts into our hands the agency to participate in the communities we live in. Autobiography is a risk, but isn't it a necessary one?

Returning to the problem of exposure, during the first years as a group we used the strategy of writing but not signing; the signature was that of the group. This privacy gave us the freedom for many forbidden stories to be shared. But what happens in the step after, when the writer wants to offer the writing of their life as their artistic work? In a context like the one I described, autobiography risks being read in the most superficial, gossipy, insensible way. How can the writer of autobiography be protected from this danger, as well as transmit an attitude of ethical and epistemological stance? How can the reader understand that the only way to gain entry to the other's territory is to touch themselves, and that it is precisely the singularity of this experience that is so valuable in autobiography? How can autobiography teach readers to read autobiography?

> There was an attic in the house. One time I climbed up to it on a ladder and discovered it was full of old comic books, magazines and books. My mother said my father used to like reading before they got married. That's where I learned to love reading, up in that attic, but my father would beat us when he found us there, he said it was dangerous, so we had to do it behind his back. When I was fifteen, they organized a sweet fifteen party, and I hated it. I had to wear a pink dress with a big bow in the back, and pose for pictures, and talk with the grownups. That day they didn't let me play with my brothers and sisters. And then when I was sixteen, my teacher at school had us write a story, and when I handed mine in she said I had copied it. Every time I write something, I always remember that. After school ended I worked two years in a restaurant because my father didn't want me to go to college, but I applied, and since I didn't have enough money to pay for veterinary science, which was what I wanted, I chose languages. And then when I got accepted, I thought: *how am I going to tell my father, my father is going to kill me*. But he didn't, and now he even asks how am I doing with my classes. (Gavilán, in Ávila, Cortés et al., 2005)

We read Kafka. For a while I have wondered what is the point of Kafka writing that long letter to his father, that is a minute and unpardoning description of the rhetoric of incommunication between father and son, whose declared purpose is "to maintain why I am afraid of you [. . . to give] an explanation of the grounds of this fear" (1979, 186). This letter is not the masochistic attitude of a cowardly son who blames all of his misfortunes on the father and does not realize it is up to him to make his life. Knowing everything the father stands for[8] and also Kafka's ability to embody oppression in order to denounce existing forms of authority, I think there is something more. My hunch is that the "Letter to the Father" is a rigorous study of all the factors that form part of an incommunicated relationship; an almost scientific study of the abyss between the self and other, the inner workings of the psychological violence that can abide in between.

> Not a word of contradiction! And the raised hand that accompanied it. (Kafka 1979, 197)

> The main thing was that the bread should be cut straight. (195)

One of the characteristics of this abyss is abstraction of the other. The son idealizes the father as this huge omnipotent oppressive figure, and the father sees only what for him should be the ideal son. What would be necessary in order to look the other in the face? How would this change our language? How would this change our reality?

> My life is a braid that has the following three strands, interwoven. The scatological: with all the darkness, all the nightmares, the unbearable pain. The "normal" life of a girl in the Colombian countryside: with its beatings, its work in the fields, its struggle to get education, the drunk father, the indolent mother, the gender conflict of a girl who is raised to be a boy . . . And finally the line of tenderness: which I am trying to recover, some kind of hope in my life. This last line is the hardest for me to find, but there is the creek I went to sit by when I had any time left from my chores as a girl, there is mountain I climb to the top of to watch the sun set when I want to die, there is writing, literature, which has saved my life. (Ávila, in Ávila, Cortés et al., 2005)

But there are qualms: How to give my story to the other? How to know that the other will not abuse my vulnerability? There is no way of knowing. We can only place our bet.

> Humberto is skinny guy who likes boys and is all teeth. He looks for ways to give them presents and invites them to his house. He works in construction. How do I know this? He goes to my father's bicycle shop to get his bike fixed. When he leaves, people tell stories. I shut my mouth and listen. One night I was on my way home, late. It was about eleven. He was coming down the

> little alley street close to my house. He got off his bike and asked me where I was coming from in a smarmy way. From the Club, I said. Without any other pretext he grabbed my crotch, over my jeans. Since I didn't protest immediately because I didn't understand what was happening—although I did get hard—he took it as a yes and said, "Let's go over there, Carlitos, and I'll suck you off." He pointed to a dark shadow cast by a bushy tree in the street that led to the river. In order to entangle his prey he offered me $800. Without thinking I said: Give me a thousand. He said he would pay me the $200 later. "Then no!" I said and ran off. I entered the house, but nobody felt my heavy breathing. (Silva, 2004, 143)

## Ethics and Politics

We take a chance on the idea that autobiography can be a form of social action. This involves understanding autobiography as something going beyond egocentrism, beyond a literary genre. Our bet is that it is a position of standing with respect to the world and to knowledge; a stance that calls the self and the other into question, and into community. Our challenge: to be fearless. We believe that truth resides in deeply listening to the shape, voice, and story of each body; and that beauty lies therein.

> We have had three horses. First we had a mare but she was stolen. The mare left us a filly which became our farm horse when she grew. Then one day it was raining really hard—when it rains around my house it rains really hard—and we told my brother ("The Brain," I call him), "Don't take the mare up to the field, it's slippery." And what did he do? He took her to the field, and riding her. The mare fell and broke her leg and we had to kill her, then skin her. We sold her to a sausage factory. Now we have a horse at the house, but he is blind. Instead of whipping him in the back, my mother would whip him in the eyes. Until he became blind. It's amazing to watch how, even though he can't see, he knows the roads around my house and into town well enough that he doesn't stumble. It's kind of cruel but it's amazing how an animal adapts to its conditions. If you take him on a new road, though, it's dangerous, he can fall. (Ávila, in Ávila, Cortés et al., 2005)

What I am pointing at, and asking for, is the undefinable space where the self-interested sensibility of autobiography is transformed into a kind of ethics. Virginia Woolf's *The Waves* (1959) profoundly transformed my perception of literature, as of reality. Through this novel, I was able to understand reality as the weave work of all of our stories—told and untold. I understood how deeply the act of giving a voice to the singularity of each subject transforms our attitude towards truth and knowledge, from monological, to dialogical, multidimensional, polyphonic. Autobiography as stance is the invitation to adopt that position, through language, because it is through language that the relationship between ourselves and the world-truth-reality is established.

> I came to the puddle. I could not cross it. Identity failed me. We are nothing, I said and fell. I was blown like a feather. I was wafted down tunnels. Then very gingerly, I pushed my foot across. I laid my hand against a brick wall. I returned very painfully drawing myself back into my body over the grey, cadaverous space of the puddle. This is life then to which I am committed. (Woolf, 1959, 64)
>
> What I call my life is not one life that I look back upon: I am not one person; I am many people, I do not altogether know who I am—Jinny, Susan, Neville, Rhoda or Louis: or how to distinguish my life from theirs. (276)

It was through language that this understanding was activated deep within my body, to the point that my individual body understood itself to be part of a larger body, alive and beating, not just in literature, but in life. The novel provoked in me the necessity of practicing ethics as the creation of a space for the multiplicity of ways in which we experience the world. There can be no truth, no community—*The Waves* taught me—unless we learn to see with many eyes, unless we learn to embody the constantly changing, eternally self-renovating rhythm of the sea.

> With intermittent shocks, sudden as the springs of a tiger, life emerges, heaving its dark crest from the sea. It is to this we are attached, to this we are bound, like bodies to wild horses. And yet we have invented devices for filling up the crevices and disguising these fissures. (Woolf, 1959, 64)
>
> . . . the joy of intercourse. I, mixed with an unknown Italian waiter—what am I? there is no stability in this world. . . . All is experiment and adventure. We are forever mixing ourselves with unknown qualities. (118)

This form of "life story" is the (multiple) counterpoint to Kafka's letter. Kafka puts all his tragic strength into showing the sterility of an incommunicated relationship, but Virginia escapes sterility by embodying the greater body of the world.

> I wasn't sent to school until I was 9 years old because I was really puny and my mother said the other girls would beat me, but it was the other way around. My younger brother was in second grade and I was in first and we walked to school a full hour at good pace. My older brother would be left to take care of us, and he was a bastard. He knew how long it took us to get home from school, and he knew we got out at 12:30, so at that time he would spit on the ground, and if the spit had dried by the time we got back, he would beat us severely. If the sun was out, too bad for us. That is how I learned to run. (Ávila, in Ávila, Cortés et al., 2005)

You spent a long time of your life without the practice of reading and writing. Are you a different person, now that you have not only passed through college but have acquired the love for literature and the need for writing? Are these two persons connected, the girl from the past, who carries this tornado of memories so hard to make sense of . . . and the girl of now, who is trying to convince herself that this story is the fiber you are made of, and that it is not a closed story, that you are not just the victim but the author of this life you are telling? You have a gift for using words in a way that not only sends shivers up a reader's spine, but also caresses your own wound. "Saved" by the fact that one day a literary critic read your writing and said, "*This is the pain of Colombia; this is not her tragedy, it is Colombia's.*" You are a metaphor, you discover, at twenty-six. But you are also not a metaphor. This is where your writing comes from.

> I don't know why but I love water. We live at the entrance of town, and as child I loved going to the country to help my grandmother with the farm chores. Then Grandmother died and then we had *toque de queda*[9] for ten years, so it was really dangerous to go out at night. We were six children but I am a triplet and one of my sisters died at birth. Perhaps this is why I have always felt a sense of insatisfaction, incompleteness about everything I do. I can be with my family, and having a good time, but there is some part of me that is always empty. Then, in 2000, when Bill Clinton came to Colombia for a day, the guerilla came

> down from the mountains and took over my town. My six-year-old little sister was killed that day. She was playing in the street. The government gave us money to compensate for her death. So now there are only four of us. We were paid for her death. When I heard the name of the group, *Lenguaje y paz,* I was immediately interested. Coming from La Uvita, Boyacá, I feel that I have looked violence in the face. (López, in Ávila, Cortés et al., 2005)

I want to be a giant pair of lips to kiss your wounded body. These stories are not looking for compassion. Not having been bold enough for suicide, they seek only to embrace life and be looked at in all their beauty and their courage.

> We have seen violence in the face.

Suely Rolnik is a Brazilian psychoanalyst and theorist who proposes "micropolitics" as a vital strategy of "inserting oneself in the tension between the dominant political cartography, with its relative stability, and that of sensible reality, in constant flux" (Rolnik, 2010, 123). Macropolitical action is a confrontational "battle for the redistribution of power and agencies" (123) based on the preexisting representations of identity; micropolitical action is "achieved through sensation . . . taking in the alterity of the world as a diagram of forces that affect our bodies in their capacity to resonate. In this process, the other is integrated like a molecule into the sensitive flesh of our bodies, and becomes a living presence" (125) that expands perception and produces new definitions of who we are and our relation with the world. Micropolitical action is a creative act that activates our potency of invention and renovates our capacity for resonance with each other and with regards to the demands that life is constantly setting (Rolnik, 2010).

The violence of nation is a prism we have all experienced from different sides. By telling our side of the prism we lay claim to the country we live in. By telling stories we re-member the broken body of nation. In this way we make a House of Language, we recognize ourselves as a part of the world. But the world is so wounded. Our tactic is to touch the wound of the world in each of our bodies, in each of our stories. Touching the wound of the world we touch the other; it is then that the word "peace" comes into play. Only linked to a body—to that body's story—and to the contact between bodies, does this vaporous word have any texture, any capacity for resonance and creative potency. We call this gamble "Language and Peace."

## *Postscript*

And myself? Behind the hand who writes there is always a strangled story. How does the voice of the research director and teacher of these students fit in? I would like to say I have grown out of the brown earth like a tree and fallen on the ground like a ripe mango. I would like to mention memories of dirty feet and a mother with hips wide enough to be the mother of a million orphans. But there is none of that. I am embarrassed to confess my previous ignorance of the people my students are. I have always been as of a different world, a world that I felt made me apolitical.

I grew up on the privileged side. I am a ghost whose origins date back to that Gothic German fairy tale called economic and cultural colonization, and its abuses. When I ask myself why I had never wanted to think about politics, I guess the answer is natural. It did not seem necessary. But also, as I grew older, this word felt weighed down by a feeling of Guilt. I didn't want my story to continue the pattern of injustice. I have wanted to cut a different path.

My first twenty years of study took place in "the best" learning institutions, which had no regard for the social context in which we lived. I was the recipient of a conception of knowledge that taught me to think only of my personal progress, to forget about social differences, and to erase any questions about what was my place in the world. As a literature student I wondered, "If the writing of literature fed from the world, how could the study of literature return something to the world, through its experiences of freedom in language?"

Political awakening began through my legs, through my ass, and all of my body. Walking, dancing, loving, defying prescribed borders, I became a part of a city I had never felt a part of. The city led to the land, traveling to the mountains, to the country, to the jungle. I met people whose language I could barely understand. As I learned to make my own voice softer, I began to come aware of the brokenness and beauty all around me. The teacher in me was born the day I realized how much I had to learn, how tight the limits of my world were. Pedagogy has been a way of giving back the world and healing a wound that has been there since before I was born.

*Lenguaje y Paz* is the name we have given to an institutional research project, but it is also life meaning, life project, the practice of literature as a radical form of ethics. It is the building of a house and a community, in language, on the terms of desire, for all of those who did not have one. It is a life boat, my own. A political becoming deeply connected to all of our wounds, the finding of a place around the wound that we all share. I give thanks for the fortune of having come into contact with these lives, these stories. By being close to them, I am part of a social body, no longer a ghost.

## Notes

1. In the landscapes of the Oriental Plains or Llanos region of Colombia, the sun gets intensely red at sunrise and sunset. This is called "the deer's sun."

2. A system of wall construction that involves a structure of wood or bamboo sticks covered with adobe.

3. This is a cousin of Brer Rabbit.

4. In the plains of Colombia it is said there is a large fireball that chases men and women who walk around late at night. It can only be scared off by slapping one's belt against the ground and saying all the bad words one can think of.

5. The Whistler turned into a phantom because he killed his father. He appears to lonely men and women walking late at night and scares them with his vibrant whistle: "zui" "zui" "zui."

6. A traditional legend from many parts of Colombia. She is a woman who has lost her baby and goes around haunting the river beds at night, in search of children to steal. Gloria Anzaldúa (1999) says she is one of the syncretic transformations of one of the ancient Mexican goddesses.

7. Another legend. The story of a woman with only one leg who goes around seducing men and taking them away.

8. "In the language of psychoanalysis, the Law of the Father or the paternal metaphor cannot be taken at its word. It is a process of substitution and exchange

that inscribes a normative, normalizing place for the subject; but that metaphoric access to identity is exactly the place of prohibition and repression, a conflict of authority" (Bhabha 2002, 52).

9. This is when an armed group forces a whole town to stay inside their homes after 6 p.m.

## References

Anderson, Linda. 2001. *Autobiography*. London: Routledge.

Anzaldúa, Gloria. 1999. *Borderlands/La frontera*. San Francisco: Aunt Lute.

Ávila, Adela, Libardo Cortés et al. 2005. Antología autobiográfica. In *Informe de investigación: Proyecto Lenguaje y Paz*. Unpublished document. Tunja: Universidad Pedagógica y Tecnológica de Colombia.

Bakhtin, Mikhail. 1986. The problem of speech genres. In M. M. Bakhtin, *Speech genres and other late essays*, trans. Vern W. McGee; eds. Caryl Emerson and Michael Holquist. Austin: University of Texas Press.

Barthes, Roland. 1975. *The pleasure of the text*. New York: Hill and Wang.

——. 1977. *Roland Barthes by Roland Barthes*. New York: Hill and Wang.

Bhabha, Homi. 2002. *The location of culture*. New York: Routledge.

Cixous, Hélène. 1991. *Coming to writing and other essays*. London: Harvard University Press.

——. 1994. *Rootprints: Memory and life writing*. London: Routledge.

de Man, Paul. 2001. Autobiography as de-facement. In *Deconstruction: A reader*, ed. Martin MacQuillan, 171–75. New York: Routledge.

Derrida, Jacques, and Geoffrey Bennington. 1993. *Jacques Derrida*. Chicago: University of Chicago Press.

Epp, Ellie. 2005. Speaking bodies: Understanding language as embodied. Embodiment web worksite. http://www.ellieepp.com/mbo/bodies/workshops .html (accessed April 1, 2014).

Heidegger, Martin. 1971. *On the way to language*. New York: Harper and Row.

Kafka, Franz. 1979. Letter to the father. *The basic Kafka*, intro. Erich Heller, 185–235. New York: Washington Square.

Ker Conway, Jill. 1999. *When memory speaks: Exploring the art of autobiography*. New York: Vintage .

Mirriam-Goldberg, Caryn, and Janet Tallman, eds. 2007. *The power of words: A transformative language arts reader*. Freedom, ME: Transformative Language Arts Network Press.

Molano, Alfredo. 2010. La gente no habla en conceptos a menos que quiera esconderse. *Revista de Estudios Colombianos*, 36:3–6. http://www.colombianistas.org/Portals/0/Revista/REC-36/4.REC_36_AlfredoMolano.pdf (accessed February 1, 2014).

Molloy, Silvia. 1996. *Acto de presencia: la escritura autobiográfica en hispanoamérica*. México, D.F.: Colegio de Mexico.

Páramo, Guillermo. 2001. La belleza está en los ojos de quien la mira o la tragedia de no ver belleza en el propio rostro. *Hojas del Farfacá*, 2:2–6.

Rolnik, Suely. 2010. Furor de archivo. *Estudios Visuales*, 7:116–30. http://estudiosvisuales.net/revista/pdf/num7/08_rolnik.pdf (accessed February 1, 2014).

Silva, Juan Carlos. 2004. "En la corriente del río: fotogramas." *Revista La Palabra*, 12:141–46.

Wolf, Christa. 1995. Speaking of Buchner. In Christa Wolf, *The author's dimension: Selected works*. Chicago: Chicago University Press.

Woolf, Virginia. 1959. *The waves*. New York: Harcourt Brace.

# Snapshot

## Richard Hodgson, Midland, Texas

*Writer, storyteller, and workshop facilitator for elders*

> "The students worked hard for me because they liked the time to speak about their own lives. For them as well as me, TLA helps us see and understand our dreams." —Richard Hodgson

In recent years, I have been busy putting together two books of poetry and working on a novel. This follows giving creative writing workshops in senior citizen centers in area communities. I traveled with my wooden bucket of words to give them ideas in writing, and we all had fun. Many of them realized, through the classes, that their history or memories in life are important to many others that they do not know. The classes became sessions of writing their memoirs and they enjoyed it a lot more than even I expected.

In the Philippines I gave a three-hour talk at Philippine Normal University, just outside of Butuan, on TLA, American literature (Mark Twain, Stafford, Bly, etc.), creativity, and told a few stories. I was amazed at the politeness and the interest shown by the 500 or so students in the audience. One thing I felt good about was I had them laughing, crying, cheering, and no one left the talk or fell asleep.

I was a substitute teacher for a period of time in grade school, middle school, and high school, where I had the opportunity to tell stories and got the students interested enough that they had the opportunity to relate stories in their lives. The students worked hard for me because they liked the time to speak about their own lives. For them as well as for me, TLA helps us see and understand our dreams.

# Snapshot

## Scott Youmans, Philadelphia, Pennsylvania, and Boulder, Colorado

*Seminarian, web consultant, writer, and facilitator*

The practice of transformative language arts isn't something I leave at home when I work as a Web consultant through Youmans Media, or as membership director of the Church of the Larger Fellowship. As a champion of right livelihood, I use what I learn to both choose my clients and inform how I engage with them. Through my presence and modeling of right livelihood and right communication, I have created positive change on the teams and individuals I collaborate with on a daily basis. That, to me, is a form of TLA in daily practice.

After graduating with a master's in TLA, I developed ideas from my research into programs that I offered to religious communities, men's groups, and at a local wellness center, all of which allowed me to share my gifts while offering participants opportunities for emotional wholeness, creative expression, and enjoyment. Now, after lengthy discernment, I am in my first year of seminary at Starr King School for the Ministry where my TLA background informs how I engage and embody my religious studies. As a Unitarian Universalist minister, I see TLA being a vital part of my ministry. I offer sessions on cosmology, embodying king energy, and right livelihood at the annual Power of Words conference, through online classes with the TLA Network, and in my faith and local communities.

I love how staying engaged with TLA brings me into contact with a diverse collection of artists, musicians, writers, and performers whose voices inspire change in the world and in my heart.

www.thisenergeticman.com

# 10

# Deep Connection

## *Healing Self, Others, and Nature through Transformative Language Arts*

Brian W. Sunset

## Opening Up

Forty-five years old and severely depressed, "Sherry" (name changed to maintain confidentiality) was admitted to the mental health treatment center where I worked after a failed suicide attempt.

While reading through Sherry's chart one afternoon, I discovered that one of her interests was poetry writing. So I knocked on her door, introduced myself, and mentioned our common interest in poetry writing.

> "I don't write much anymore," she said, her eyes fixed to the ceiling of her darkened room.
>
> "If you'd like," I said, "I know a word game we can play. You draw words from a basket and use them to make poems."
>
> "We can play now," said Sherry, "if it only takes a few minutes." She cast me a cautious glance.

So I took a seat at a table in the dining area, where we had agreed to meet, and waited for her to emerge, which she did about ten minutes later.

While seated at the table, we picked out words from a bowl and arranged them into poems. After sharing our creations, Sherry chatted briefly about her interest in poetry writing. She'd started writing poetry as a child, she told me, but stopped when her mom found them and told her she didn't think they were very good. Several days later, Sherry, who was spending more time outside her room, sought me out and handed me a poem she had found in a magazine. The poem dealt with issues of separation and loss, much like those she had dealt with in the loss of her marriage. About a week after that, she shared with me a poem that she herself had written. In it, she spoke about her desire to embrace change in her life.

Prior to her discharge, Sherry related to me how, during her stay at the center, she had begun to write poetry again. Then she handed me a poem in which she spoke about her desire to create new possibilities. I asked her whether poetry writing had been helpful in her recovery process. She nodded. "It helped break up the log jam," she said.

Since my experience working with Sherry, I have learned some of the reasons why expressive writing is a healthy way to break up emotional log jams. According to James Pennebaker (1990), writing about one's deepest thoughts and feelings can lead to improved moods, greater physical health, heightened immune function, and a more positive outlook, by which he means, I assume, a certain optimism, confidence, and resiliency as opposed to a lack of such qualities. According to Samuels and Lane, "a person in prayer, a person making art, and a person healing all have the same physiology, the same brain wave patterns, and the same states of consciousness" (1992, 1–2). When one is making art—in this case, writing poetry—the physiology that results is like the physiology of prayer and meditation, which promotes deep relaxation and healing.

Laura Cerwinske (1999) likens the expressive writing process to a river, in which the free circulation of blood leads to the development of oxygen, which produces the nutrients that produce the blood. This cyclical process, she says, engages the body's restorative mechanism. But when the river is clogged, the system breaks down, diminishing wholeness. Troubling thoughts, difficult emotions, memories of traumatic events—all of these can clog the system, therefore obstructing this up-and-out process. The repression of emotion, according to Pennebaker, can actually lead to heart disease, distress, and other major and minor illnesses. "Like other stressors," he says, "inhibition can affect immune function, the action of the heart and vascular systems, and even the biochemical workings of the brain and nervous systems" (1990, 2).

## Roots of Poetic Healing

Not surprisingly, modern studies often validate what people of Earth-centered cultures have known instinctively for a very long time. Ancient shamans, in fact, were probably the first individuals to use words in a healing capacity. According to Beck and Walters (1977), "the shaman was often an all-around sacred practitioner: a mystic, a doctor, an herbalist, a diagnostician, a hunter, a singer, a storyteller, an artist, and a person of knowledge" (103). To the shaman, though, it was not only the herbs administered to the sick person that aided healing, it was the mysterious words handed down by the deities that were spoken, sung, or chanted to the patient or over the healing herb.

According to Samuels and Lane, the "place" to which the shaman must travel to snatch down healing words is the "place where there is no time and space, where natural laws don't apply in the usual way. And that is the place of shamanic healing" (1992, 99). It is also the place to which the creative arts give us access. If shamans functioned in a number of capacities in early societies, poets functioned in a number of capacities too. These included magician, prophet, historian, priest, and entertainer at noble courts and religious festivals. They also functioned to advance the language, to convey the ethics and morals of a society, and to communicate mythic and universal truths. Poets were well respected and highly regarded. According to Kevin Crossley-Holland (1980), "primitive societies venerated poets second only to their leaders. A poet had the power to name and so to control; he was, literally, the living memory of a group or tribe who would perpetuate their history in song; his inspiration was god given and he was in effect a medium" (190).

Poetry appears in the mythic traditions of many cultures. The ancient Greeks, for example, are believed to be among the earliest peoples to recognize the connection between words and feelings and poetry and healing. The god Apollo was at once god of light and patron of mathematics, music, healing, and poetry. In the Norse *Mead of Poetry* we learn that the sage Kvasir was created as a sign of peace following a battle between the gods of the sky and the gods of the Earth. Among other qualities, Kvasir had the ability to listen to people's problems, responding in such a way that "he made gods and men, giants and dwarfs feel that they had been helped to answer their own question" (Crossley-Holland, 1980, 26).

## Embracing the Questions

In the journaling groups that I facilitate at the hospital and in other environments, the writing process often begins with a question. This practice is inspired not only by Kvasir's example, but by my long-held interest in dream work and the approach of Jungian therapist-analyst Strephon Kaplan Williams (1980). In the *Jungian-Senoi Dreamwork Manual*, he states, "It is more important to ask the right question than to receive a right answer" (170).

In my groups, we enter the writing process through a response to a central question. For example, "Where is a place in nature where you feel connected, or at peace, and how do you connect with that place by way of the senses?" I try to pose questions that elicit pleasant memories. The question above evokes rich responses. Examples include *my grandparents' farm and the aroma of freshly mown hay; the desert and all the stars visible at night* and *the ocean and the texture of the sand beneath my feet*. Individuals then create their own questions and utilize these as the starting point for their writing. Questions might be, for example, "What do I remember about my grandparents' farm and the aroma of freshly mown hay?" or "How do I feel when I am in the desert gazing up at the stars?" When we ask questions, we make room for the type of self-exploration and introspection, and the attitude of curiosity and openness, that are so essential to the transformative language arts (TLA) process.

## A Consideration of Terms

I would like, at this point, to provide a brief examination of words that I have found to be particularly useful in my own TLA practice—*heal*, *transform*, and *connect*.

The word *heal* derives from the Anglo-Saxon word *haelan*, to heal. Related words include *hale*, meaning in good health or sound, and *holy*. *Transform* derives from the French *transformer*, which means to change the form of, to give a new form to, or to metamorphose. Whereas the word *heal* implies restoration to a state of wholeness or health, *transform* implies movement toward a new state of being. The word *connect* comes from the Latin word *con* (together) plus *nectere* (bind), and means *to fasten together, to join or unite,* and *to establish communication with* (Thatcher, 1971).

One of the goals of my own TLA practice is to cultivate people's sense of wholeness. A second is to create the conditions whereby transformation is possible. And a third is to build meaningful connections between group participants. These terms, of course, should not be thought of solely in the human-to-human context, but in the much broader context of the human being, which is the ecological context. Though many of us would prefer to operate outside of this frame of reference, influenced as we are by institutions—religious, political, and economic—which tend to support anthropocentric attitudes and practices, in reality we cannot operate outside this ecological frame. As people of Earth-centered traditions have known, and modern scientists have now begun to recognize, everything in nature is connected. In the words of physicist Fritjof Capra (2000):

> The basic oneness of the universe is not only the central characteristic of the mystical experience, but is also one of the most important revelations of modern physics. It becomes apparent at the atomic level and manifests itself more and more as one penetrates deeper into matter, down into the realm of subatomic particles. (131)

Thus, one way to restore the human being is to move from anthropocentric to ecocentric attitudes, recognizing once again our sacred interconnection with all living things. Furthermore, we must begin to operate out of this new, ancient awareness as if our very existence depended upon it, which in reality it does. TLA, or *eco-TLA*, as I refer to my practice, is ideally suited for this task because it promotes the healing of individuals and their communities, including the broader ecological communities, of which they are a part.

## Core Tenets

How does eco-TLA support the process of healing, transformation, and connection? To support this process, I operate by the following core tenets: First, *everyone in the group has something unique and valuable to share.* As part of the group, people announce their place in the family of things through the words they speak, the poems they share, and even through the simple act of announcing their name at the start of every group session.

In the Writing for Personal Growth group that I facilitate at the hospital, I place a cardboard cutout of a sun, which I have decorated with orange, yellow, and red tissue paper, at the center of the table, around which the participants are seated. Raised slightly at the edges, it whirls when patients set it in motion, which I ask them to do. When it stops spinning, I explain that the sun functions on two levels. First, I say, the rays point in every direction, reminding us that we all have something valuable to share. Second, I explain that the sun symbolizes the inner light, or innate wisdom, which I believe we all possess inside us. And the writing process, I say, connects us with that core wisdom.

The second core tenet is that *we operate from a place of curiosity, rather than critique.* The above example of Sherry, whose mother found her poems and dismissed them as not very good, illustrates why critique is not part of the writing groups that I facilitate. Critique—as compared to questions—can cut off the creative flow at the very time an individual is beginning to open up.

Operating from a place of curiosity, people reflect upon what they have written—for example, feelings and emotions it evokes, discoveries or insights it provides, or questions it provokes. When finished, the writer may invite reflections from the group. Listeners may share a detail from the piece that spoke to them in some way, ask a question about something expressed in the piece, or share briefly a memory or association that the piece evoked in them. The curiosity model, because it doesn't rely upon critique, supports the goal of building trust among group members and contributes to the atmosphere of safety and security in the group.

The third core tenet is that *everything in nature is divine.* This tenet is reflected in the way in which everyone in the group is treated with integrity and respect. We listen deeply, speak from the heart, and practice confidentiality. Respect extends beyond the human community to include Raven, Mountain, River—indeed, anything we bring into the process through the imagination, experience, memory, or dreams.

One way that we extend this respect to other natural things is by the simple act of including them in our consideration. For example, I might ask group participants to reflect upon an animal with which they feel connected. Once everyone has named an animal—it might be a mythic animal, a power animal, or other animal with which they have had a direct experience—we use the writing process to explore that connection. Useful questions include *What qualities do I admire about Squirrel?*, for example, and *How can I integrate these qualities into my life?* or *What might Squirrel like to tell me, if it could speak in human language?*

Individuals can write prose, poems, dialogues, even lists of words—whichever approach feels right or achievable at the time. Other topics that generate rich writing include insects, such as Dragonfly or Honey Bee; weather features, such as wispy clouds or thunder storms; and landscapes, such as deserts or mountains. The point is to include these Others in our writing and, through this process, to reflect upon and honor their presence in our lives.

The fourth core tenet, *we are all connected*, is reflected in the words of Walt Whitman, in his poem "We Two, How Long We Were Fool'd." He says,

> We are Nature, long have we been absent, but
> now we return,
> We become plants, trunks, foliage, roots, bark,
> We are bedded in the ground,
> We are rocks,
> We are oaks, we grow in the openings side by side.

Like Whitman, I believe that we are nature and that we are intricately connected. In nature we have the example of Spider weaving her web of connections, each strand relying upon the other for its tensile strength. In my practice, I liken myself to Spider weaving webs of connection between group members. In group, therefore, participants are given regular opportunities to write and share. They are also encouraged to find meaning in the various symbols, lines, words, and images expressed in their writing. In group, we practice careful, respectful listening—to self as well as others—and commit ourselves to full participation.

## The Divine in Nature

The attitude of the divinity of nature and sacred interconnection is one of the essential philosophies of eco-TLA and is grounded in Eastern as well as

Western philosophical traditions. In Shinto philosophy, for example, everything in nature, including rocks, trees, birds, water, and insects, is infused with divine spirit, or *kami*. In Western philosophy, too, there is a basis for such a *kami* belief. Emerson speaks about the concept of the "over-soul." "The heart in thee," he says, "is the heart of all; not a valve, not a wall, not an intersection is there anywhere in nature, but one blood rolls uninterruptedly an endless circulation through all men, as the water of the globe is all one sea, and, truly seen, its tide is one" (Emerson, 1968, 209–10).

Hegel, too, seems to support such a *kami* attitude. According to Paul Redding (2002), in Hegel's view "the mind of God becomes actual only via the minds of his creatures, who serve as its vehicle. It is as distributed bearers of this developing self-consciousness of God that those finitely-embodied inhabitants of the universe—we humans—can be such 'finite-infinites.'" Underlying Hegel's attitude seems to be a certain pantheistic assumption similar to Emerson's and that of Shinto philosophy.

The idea of interconnection is reflected in Jung's concept of *unus mundus*, or "one world." According to Jung's philosophy, there exists in nature an unconscious transcendental reality that unites psychic and physical realities. This reality operates independently of the human psyche, manifesting inwardly as psychological archetypes and outwardly as the archetypal laws of nature (McFarlane, 2000). In Hindu philosophy, *Brahman* is the thread unifying the web of life, and the source of all things:

> He on whom the sky, the earth, and the atmosphere
> Are woven, and the wind, together with all life-breaths,
> Him alone knows as the one Soul.
>
> (*Mundaka Upanishad*, 2.2.5)

That we are all united by a transcendental reality may seem implausible to some individuals. To individuals of many native societies, however, the notion that we are all interconnected is a core belief. According to Beck and Walters (1977), "One of the most important concepts Native American tribal people share with respect to the sacred is that all things in the universe are dependent on each other" (105). That such attitudes have a basis also in Western philosophy may give some individuals the permission they seek to shift away from an anthropocentric worldview to one that embraces the philosophy that all things have intrinsic value and should be treated with dignity and respect.

In order for us to have truly meaningful encounters with other beings, however, we must believe that such interactions are possible. According to psychotherapist Philip Chard (1994), "Blending with nature invokes new possibilities: those that can be grown from the human spirit and those that can be reaped from the emotional and spiritual essences of animals, plants, elements, and natural forces" (75). David Abram (1996) says, "Only by affirming the animateness of perceived things do we allow our words to emerge directly from the depths of our ongoing reciprocity with the sensuous world of nature" (56).

But how do we cultivate such a *kami* attitude in our current anthropocentric society, which seems to reduce everything other-than-human to its economic value? One way to cultivate this attitude is to seek the transformation and healing not of human beings alone but of the whole world of nature, which binds us together into one sacred expression of life. I will now suggest some practical ways to support the process of healing, transformation, and connection through use of the eco-TLA process.

## Some Tools for Eco-TLA

Poetry stems, engaging the senses, and writing from the perspective of other living things are among the many tools that I employ to help individuals reconnect with self, others, and nature. Poetry stems are poetic lines used to elicit brief responses—oral or written—from participants in transformative writing groups. Examples of poetry stems include "In times of silver rain" (Langston Hughes) and "I am one who" (Matsuo Bashō). The line "I am one who" has evoked such responses as "I am one who likes to laugh," "I am one who loves the ocean," and "I am one who feels sad." In my groups, poetry stems are first spoken aloud—and not written down—to promote a direct, spontaneous heart-to-mouth connection.

Among the goals of poetry stems is to give people an opportunity to announce their presence in the group and to speak their truth. In my groups, however, individuals are never pressured to share and may always pass. But even when passing, individuals receive validation from the group because in this case they are claiming their right not to share. I have found, however, that over the course of several sessions individuals electing not to share initially often do share. Flowers open up at their own pace, and conditions must be right for them to do so.

I remember a session that I was facilitating for male inmates at the county jail. We had started out with the poetry stem "I am one who," and on the first pass around the circle, one man responded, "I am one who does not want to do this silly exercise." The group laughed, but in fact I was delighted with that man's response. We continued around the circle several times more using that question, and with each successive pass, responses grew closer to the bone. Not surprisingly, the man who had started out from an authentic place already went on to write poems that were equally authentic.

Whole poems, or individual lines selected from them by group participants, can also be utilized as springboards into expressive writing experiences. Poems that have worked well in my groups include "I Have Roads in Me," by Jimmy Santiago Baca; sections of "Fast Speaking Woman," by Anne Waldman; and "My Tree," by Rolf Jacobsen.

"My Tree" is an excellent poem to promote insight and awareness of the importance of trees in our lives. I ask participants to think of a tree with which they feel connected through memory, experience, or imagination. It might be a tree that they planted as a child, one growing in a park or other setting, or a mythic tree, such as the world tree. Then I ask them to list some of the qualities of their tree that they appreciate or admire. Oaks are often named for their patient growth and strength, willows for their flexibility and resiliency, and redwoods for their enormous stature and their ability to gaze far off into the distance. As part of this process, I ask participants to consider some ways in which to integrate these qualities into their own way of being.

When the writing process begins, participants may write about their tree from their own perspective, they may write a letter to their tree expressing what they appreciate or admire about it, or they may even write a poem as if from the tree's perspective. Following one of my tree sessions at the hospital a patient felt so moved by her connection with her tree—it was an old apple tree growing in her grandparents' backyard—that she painted a picture of it and handed it to me as a gift. At the bottom of her picture she included a line from the Rolf Jacobsen poem "My Tree." I still have her painting taped to the wall above my desk.

In a variation of this session, I hang up images of trees—from magazines, picture books, or other media—and ask participants to select a tree to which they feel drawn, or one they simply happen to like. We use these images as the basis for further writing.

Images, in fact, provide great opportunities for exploration, reflection, and writing. These can be postcard images, images of diatoms or other microscopic life forms (old issues of *National Geographic* and coffee-table books are great sources for these), or images of landscapes. When selecting images for use as writing prompts, I try to select those that evoke emotions and provide ample narrative opportunities. Other evocative writing prompts include items from nature, such as sand dollars or stones, and aromas. Aroma vials—including rosemary, chocolate, cinnamon, or coffee—stimulate the olfactory sense but also the sense of taste. Through the memories evoked, they can lead us into a whole palette of experiences about which to write.

## Deep Connections

The process of writing from the perspective of another being—human or other-than-human—has great potential to cultivate a sense of connection between writer and subject. For, if you are to do an effective job of writing as if inside the skin—or *bark*—of another being, you must grow as close as possible to that subject and to the greatest extent see the world from its perspective.

In my Writing Our Relationship with Trees workshop, we move from an initial description of trees—noting, for example, the color and shape of their leaves, the sounds they make when the wind moves through their branches, or the texture of their bark—to a deeper identification with a chosen tree. We imagine, for example, what the tree's experience of the world might be, listening, as it were, to its story. Where is it growing and how vigorously? What do the notches and marks on its trunk tell us about its history? Part of this process includes selecting a tree and spending time with it over the period of several hours, days, or weeks. Goals include cultivating a relationship with the tree, first through observation, and then deepening one's relationship with it by viewing the world as if from its perspective. If the tree had eyes, for instance, what might it see? What is its relationship with other life forms living in its vicinity? How might it feel when faced with the prospect of being felled by a human being? We can approach this process in many different ways. And then, in an imaginative leap, we practice listening to the tree and write about that experience.

This is not such an unusual practice if you believe that everything in nature is infused with spirit, as many people of Earth-centered traditions believe. In techno-industrial cultures, however, we act as if the only beings with the capacity to communicate are humans, and we often treat other life forms as if they are nothing more than inert matter under the dominion of humankind. In the words of Tatanga Mani, or Walking Buffalo, "did you know that trees talk? Well they do. They talk to each other, and they'll talk to you too, if you listen . . . I have learned a lot from trees: sometimes about the weather, sometimes about animals, sometimes about the Great Spirit" (McLuhan, 1971, 23).

In Writing Our Relationship with Trees, listening to trees involves quieting oneself and becoming receptive to what your tree is trying to tell you through your whole being. Its "words" might come to you through images arising in your mind, through what you sense, perceive, or feel when the wind sets the tree's branches in motion, or through the aroma or texture of the pitch seeping from its bark. Listening to trees, or any other natural thing, for that matter, does not rely upon human language, but is enabled by the senses. According to David Abram (1996), "Ultimately, it is not human language that is primary, but rather the sensuous, perceptual life-world, whose wild, participatory logic ramifies and elaborates itself in language" (84).

Our experience of trees, of course, must be translated into poetic language, and, as part of that process, we rely upon our capacity to be creative. Outgrowths of this process include increasing our capacity for empathy and compassion for trees, and broadening our conception of community to include them, as well as other living things.

Below is a poem written by a participant in one of my Writing Our Relationship with Trees workshops. In it, the poet uses her imagination and insights gained through spending time with her tree, to speak as if from its perspective.

**I'm a Mighty Douglas Fir**

*Karen Jackson*

I feel raindrops gently touching my branches
The sun rays make the rain glisten like teardrops
on my branches.

I'm a Mighty Douglas Fir.

I feel the birds building their nests
As they sing out their beautiful songs.

I'm a Mighty Douglas Fir.

The crows bark.
The squirrels scamper about
Tickling my roots and making me happy.

I'm a Mighty Douglas Fir.

I live through winter after winter
When the wind howls and bends my branches,
And the snowfall weighs me down,

Yet I Live on . . .

## Closing Thoughts

It is in the context of this community of others—including the landscapes in which we live, move, and breathe—that we embrace and express who we are, connecting with those other sentient beings with whom we share this planet. Through eco-TLA, people can discover and explore their own unique voice, bringing forth and embracing that which is most true and authentic about themselves and assuming their place in the family of all earthly beings.

# References


Abram, David. 1996. *The spell of the sensuous: Perception and language in a more-than-human world.* New York: Pantheon.

Beck, Peggy V., and Anna L. Walters. 1977. *The sacred: Ways of knowledge, sources of life.* Tsaile (Navaho Nation), AZ: Navaho Community College Press.

Capra, Fritjof. 2000 [1975]. *The tao of physics: An exploration of the parallels between modern physics and eastern mysticism.* Boston: Shambhala.

Cerwinske, Laura. 1999. *Writing as a healing art: The transforming power of self-expression.* New York: Berkeley/Penguin Putnam.

Chard, Philip. 1994. *The healing earth: Nature's medicine for the troubled soul.* Minocqua, WI: North Word.

Crossley-Holland, Kevin. 1980. *The Norse myths.* London: Andre Deutsch.

Emerson, Ralph Waldo. 1968. The over-soul. In *Ralph Waldo Emerson: Essays and Journals*, ed. L. Mumford. New York: Nelson Doubleday.

McFarlane, T. J. 2000. Quantum physics, depth psychology, and beyond. http://www.integralscience.org/psyche-physis.html (accessed April 2013).

McLuhan, T. C., ed. 1971. *Touch the earth: A self-portrait of Indian existence.* New York: Promontory.

Pennebaker, James W. 1990. *Opening up: The healing power of expressing emotions.* New York: Guilford.

Redding, P. 2002. Georg Wilhelm Friedrich Hegel. In *The Stanford Encyclopedia of Philosophy*, (summer ed.), ed. Edward N. Zalta. http://plato.stanford.edu/archives/sum2002/entries/hegel/ (accessed March 2014).

Samuels, Michael, and Mary Rockwood Lane. 1992. *Creative healing: How to heal yourself by tapping your hidden creativity.* San Francisco: HarperCollins.

Thatcher, V. S. 1971. *The new Webster encyclopedic dictionary of the English language.* Chicago: Consolidated.

Williams, Strephon Kaplan. 1980. *Jungian-Senoi dreamwork manual.* Berkeley, CA: Journey.

# Sources for Poems Cited Plus Additional Resources for Poems

Baca, Jimmy Santiago. 1999. I have roads in me. In *Set this book on fire! Poems by Jimmy Santiago Baca.* Mena, AR: Cedar Hill.

Bly, Robert, ed. 1980. *News of the universe: Poems of twofold consciousness.* San Francisco: Sierra Club.

Bly, Robert, Roger Greenwald, and Robert Hedin, eds. 2001. My tree. In *The roads have come to an end now: Selected and last poems of Rolf Jacobsen.* Port Townsend, WA: Copper Canyon.

Dunn, Sara, and Alan Scholefield, eds. 1991. *Poetry for the earth: A collection of poems from around the world that celebrate nature.* New York: Fawcett Columbine.

Fox, John. 1995. *Finding what you didn't lose: Expressing your truth and creativity through poem-making.* New York: Putnam.

———. 1997. *Poetic medicine: The healing art of poem-making.* New York: Jeremy P. Tarcher/Putnam.

Merrill, Christopher, ed. 1991. *The forgotten language: Contemporary poets and nature.* Salt Lake City, UT: Peregrine Smith.

Mosely, Ivo, ed. 1990. *Earth poems.* San Francisco: HarperCollins.

Price, Dorothy, ed. 1967. *Silent flowers: A new collection of Japanese haiku poems.* Tokyo: Hallmark Cards and Hokuseido.

Rampersad, Arnold, and David Roessel, eds. 1994. *The collected poems of Langston Hughes.* New York: Vintage.

Rosen, Kenneth. 1995. *Voices of the rainbow: Contemporary poetry by American Indians.* New York: Seaver/Viking.

Snyder, Gary. 1969. *Turtle Island.* New York: New Directions.

Waldman, Anne. 1996. *Fast speaking woman: Chants and essays.* San Francisco: City Light.

Whitman, Walt. 1921. We two, how long we were fool'd. In *Leaves of grass.* New York: Modern Library.

# Resources

## MA in Transformative Language Arts at Goddard College

123 Pitkin Road, Plainfield, VT 05667
800-906-8312 (Admissions)
www.goddard.edu/ma-individualized-studies/transformative-language-arts-concentration
www.Goddard.edu

**Resources through Goddard College**

- TLA Resources Center: www.TLAresources.wordpress.com
- Worlds of Change blog: www.WorldsofChange.com

# Transformative Language Arts Network (TLA Network)

576 North Palermo Road, Freedom, Maine 04941
www.TLANetwork.org

### Resources through the TLA Network

- One City One Prompt: www.OneCityOnePrompt.org
- Power of Words Conference: www.TLANetwork.org/conference/
- *Chrysalis: A Journal of Transformative Language Arts.* Scholarly, professional, and creative international journal: http://chrysalisjournal.org/
- *The Power of Words: A Transformative Language Arts Reader*: http://www.tlanetwork.org/tla-reader/
- Certification in TLA: www.TLANetwork.org/certification/

# About the Editors and Contributors

**Taína Asili** carries on the tradition of her Puerto Rican ancestors, fusing past and present struggles into one soulful and defiant voice. Her newest artistic work is with la Banda Rebelde (the Rebel Band), a six-piece ensemble based in Albany, New York. This dynamic force brings love, resistance, and ancestral remembrance to venues, festivals, conferences, and political events across the globe. Taína Asili's voice exudes strength of Spirit, filling its listeners with the fervor of freedom and inspiring audiences to dance to the movement of rebellion. Taína Asili y la Banda Rebelde released their debut album *War Cry* in 2010. www.TainaAsili.com

**Sarah W. Barlett**, AM, MPH, ScD, is an experienced writing coach and facilitator who operates Women Writing for (a) Change Vermont, LLC, a conscious community of women writing for self-discovery and social change. She also directs writinginsideVT, a weekly writing opportunity for Vermont's incarcerated women. Sarah holds advanced degrees from Harvard University in both language and health education, and is a certified mediator. Sarah's first chapbook, *Into the Great Blue: Meditations of Summer* (2011) was followed by *HEAR ME, SEE ME: Incarcerated Women Write* (2013), co-edited with Marybeth Redmond. She lives in Vermont and Massachusetts, with her writing and art supplies, dog, cat, and husband, steadfast supporter of her writing midwifery. www.sarah-w-bartlett.com

**Juliana Borrero** is a Colombian writer, translator, and researcher of writing from the body. She has a BA in literature and an MA in individualized studies with an emphasis in embodiment studies from Goddard College. She lives in Tunja, a small rural city where she is a professor and co-creator of the MA in literature at Universidad Pedagógica y Tecnológica de Colombia, a program with a special interest in research regarding the relation between language and subject, and in theorizing and promoting creation/research.

**Ruth Farmer** is an essayist, poet, fiction writer, and educator. She directs the Goddard Graduate Institute and teaches at the Community College of Vermont. Writing and learning have always been essential in her life, personally and professionally. In recent years, she has embraced dance and yoga as expressive languages that go where words cannot go.

**Yvette Angelique Hyater-Adams**, MA-TLA, is a poet, essayist, and a practitioner in applied behavioral science. She writes, teaches, and coaches using a transformative narratives-storytelling method for creative writing, personal and business histories, ghostwriting, and as a unique approach to leadership development for women and girls. She is the creator of transformative narratives coaching. www.narratives4change.com

**Callid Keefe-Perry** is a member of Rochester Monthly Meeting and travels in the Ministry—within and beyond the Friends' denomination—under the endorsement of Rochester, Farmington-Scipio Regional Meeting, and New York Yearly Meeting. He is currently sojourning at Beacon Hill Friends Meeting while he completes his doctorate in practical theology at Boston University's School of Theology. Founder of Theopoetics.net and a co-host on the progressive Christian podcast, Homebrewed Christianity, Callid has taught and performed improvised theatre, been a founder and manager of western New York's largest theater devoted to comedy, has been a consultant on the use of the arts in public school classrooms, and has also worked as a teacher of Quakerism at the Pendle Hill Retreat Center. He currently serves as the president of the Transformative Language Arts Network Council, is a grateful husband and father, and believes in the possibility of a Just World while he still lives.

**Kao Kue** is a Hmong American poet and storyteller who credits her strengths and passion for words and community building to her ancestors and foremothers. She is honored to carry their legacy of love—their sweat, their tears, and their poetry. She has witnessed her community struggle with poverty, racism, sexism, domestic violence, and alcohol and drug abuse. What has saved her and many of her community members from the destruction around them was the ability to share and create stories. As she continues to practice the art of storytelling, she hopes to provide a space for immigrant communities, especially women, to tell their stories. She believes our words will not only bring healing to our families, but it will strengthen our communities.

**Katt Lissard** teaches in Goddard's Graduate Institute and is the artistic director of The Winter/Summer Institute, an HIV/AIDS theatre project based in New York and Lesotho in southern Africa (maketheatre.org). Her essay, "Venus in Lesotho: Women, Theatre and the Collapsible Boundaries of Silence," is included in Palgrave Macmillan's recent *Feminist Popular Education in Transnational Debates*; upcoming pieces will appear in SATJ (*South African Theatre Journal*) and *Painted Bride Quarterly.*

**Caryn Mirriam-Goldberg** is the 2009–2014 Kansas Poet Laureate and author of nineteen books, including a recent collection of poetry, *Chasing Weather: Tornadoes, Tempests, and Thunderous Skies in Word and Image*, in collaboration with photographer Stephen Locke; the memoir *Poem on the Range: A Poet Laureate's Love Song to Kansas*; the novel *The Divorce Girl*; and the nonfiction book *Needle in the Bone: How a Holocaust Survivor and Polish Resistance Fighter Beat the Odds and Found Each Other*. Founder of Transformative Language Arts at Goddard College, where she teaches in the Graduate Institute, Mirriam-Goldberg leads community writing workshops widely. www.CarynMirriamGoldberg.com

**Ezra Berkley Nepon** is a Philadelphia-based writer, performer, and grassroots fundraiser. Nepon is author of the book *Justice, Justice Shall You Pursue: A History of New Jewish Agenda* (2012), and has also been published in *Grassroots Fundraising Journal, Movement Research Performance Journal, Make/Shift Magazine, Tikkun, Jewish Currents*, and more. Nepon received an

MA from Goddard College in 2012 with a thesis titled "Unleashing Power in Yiddishland and Faerieland: Spectacular Theatrical Strategies for Resilience and Resistance." www.ezraberkleynepon.wordpress.com

**James Sparrell,** PhD, is trained as a clinical/community psychologist who currently works in public schools and private practice in addition to teaching in the Goddard Graduate Institute at Goddard College. Informed by narrative therapy and years of careful listening, he has a strong belief in the power of change inherent in deep personal connection, new perspectives, and narratives that challenge dominant cultural stories. His phylogenetic interests have shifted slightly from snakes to birds and he has recently started an afterschool birding group for elementary school students.

**Brian W. Sunset** holds an MA in transformative language Arts from Goddard College and a certification in poetry therapy. He facilitates transformative language arts groups in diverse environments, including hospitals, community centers, and jails. He also facilitates Healing Landscapes and Writing Our Relationship with Trees workshops, which explore the connections between the expressive arts and deep ecology. For further information about Brian and his work, or for information about upcoming workshops and events, go to www.cascadiaahc.com.